AF413808

OUTPERFORM

THE CONSTRAINT-DRIVEN METHOD™ *to*

Outperform in Law School with a Full Life

L. Christina-M. Jackson

Published by Constraint-Driven Press
Printed in the United States of America
ISBN (paperback): 979-8-9950068-0-0 ISBN (hardcover): 979-8-9950068-1-7
Library of Congress Control Number: 2026907681

First edition

Trademark & Standards Notice
The Constraint-Driven Method™ and related framework names are trademarks of Leyo Christina Jackson. Trademark registration is pending. This book introduces the student application of the Method. Institutional adoption, formal implementation, certification, or branded program use requires written authorization. For licensing or implementation inquiries, please refer to the Contact & Resources section.

FOREWORD

Law students are often told both explicitly and implicitly that success requires total attention, unwavering commitment, and devotion. In my almost ten years of experience as Dean of Students, it is the rare student who has the luxury of boundless energy, undistracted focus, and an uninterrupted schedule. Many are parents, caregivers, full-time professionals, military members, or individuals navigating ongoing responsibilities that do not pause simply because they have enrolled in law school. Yet these students show up with determination to excel in a system that demands much from them.

Law schools can acknowledge these challenges, provide resources and structures that benefit non-traditional students and their schedules, but at the end of the day, every student must still do the work, learn the material, and demonstrate their understanding.

The Constraint-Driven Method™ speaks directly and unapologetically to them.

Ms. Jackson dismantles the myth that excellence is available only to the student with the fewest responsibilities. This book also recognizes that high performance is inseparable from wellbeing, not because wellbeing demands perfect balance, but because students cannot sustainably excel in systems that ignore their lived realities.

Drawing from her own experience, and the experiences of others who successfully navigated law school while facing real-life constraints, Ms. Jackson offers a system intentionally designed for people whose lives are already full, whose time is already spoken for, and whose wellbeing requires more than generic advice that often becomes just another demand on their limited time and energy.

What makes this book most remarkable is not only its practicality but its honesty. Ms. Jackson names what traditional legal environments often refuse to acknowledge: that exhaustion, guilt, and isolation are not signs of inability. They are predictable outcomes of attempting to perform in a structure that was not built with nontraditional students or their realities in mind. Rather than encouraging students to push harder within such a system, she shows them how to redesign performance in ways that protect cognitive health, emotional steadiness, and long-term endurance.

This book reframes constraint from something to hide or overcome into something that must be acknowledged. It demonstrates that wellbeing is not an accessory to execution but a foundational component of it. Endurance is not fueled by motivation, but by alignment: students' responsibilities, energy, and limitations must be integrated into their plan rather than pushed against. Ms. Jackson notes with clarity that high performance is not a privilege reserved for those with empty calendars or ideal conditions, but a possibility available to anyone who learns to embrace these tactics within the life they actually have.

Readers will walk away with far more than study tips. They will gain an integrated way of thinking, planning, and executing that holds under pressure, preserves wellbeing rather than trading it away, and supports success through law school and the bar exam, and in every high-stakes environment that follows. This book is both a guide and a call to action. It challenges institutions to recognize the real students who pass through their doors and to understand that wellbeing is not optional for educational excellence; it is the infrastructure that makes excellence possible.

For the nontraditional law student balancing life outside of law school, this book does more than recognize your reality. It equips you to excel within it.

Many law school guidebooks frame the experience as a matter of survival. I reject the premise that pursuing a legal education should feel like an existential threat. Even so, law school does require intention, self-awareness, and honesty about the challenges ahead. This book offers a blueprint for approaching the experience deliberately, realistically, and sustainably.

Lynn LeMoine, JD
Dean of Students
Mitchell Hamline School of Law

AUTHOR'S NOTE

This book is written for law students whose lives do not pause for school. If you are balancing law school alongside work, family, financial responsibility, caregiving, or other obligations that cannot be set aside, you are not behind—you are operating under different conditions that require different strategies.

The Constraint-Driven Method™ is a framework for achieving consistent performance in law school while carrying real-world responsibilities. It is not motivational guidance. It is an operating system: a practical approach to designing study and execution around the life you actually have, rather than the life law schools assume.

Nothing in this book constitutes legal advice. It is an educational resource grounded in observation, institutional analysis, and strategic design. Apply the Method deliberately, adapt it to your circumstances, and evaluate results against outcomes—rather than effort.

Although this book is written for students, the Constraint-Driven Method™ extends to law school academic support professionals, pipeline programs, and institutions. Formal institutional implementation follows defined standards to ensure clarity, consistency, and fidelity across contexts.

TABLE OF CONTENTS

How to Use This Book

This book is structured as a system, not a collection of tips. Some sections are intended to be read sequentially; others are designed to be revisited as conditions change. You do not need uninterrupted time or ideal circumstances to use it effectively.

The Constraint-Driven Method™ is composed of three integrated components:

- *The Five Pillars*, which explain how performance systems must be designed under constraint

- *The Ten Core Principles*, which govern day-to-day decision-making under pressure

- *The Three Operational Domains*, which define where those decisions are applied

Together, these components form a cohesive framework. While the architecture is intentional, the Method is designed for reuse and recalibration rather than one-time consumption.

- If you are early in your studies or feeling overwhelmed, begin with Part II, *Internal Endurance.*

- If you are working hard but not seeing results, focus on Part III, *Performance Execution.*

- If effort is not translating into opportunity, Part IV, *Relational and Institutional Leverage* may be the missing element.

When something stops working, the correct response is not to add more techniques, but to diagnose the breakdown. The Method is designed to stabilize performance first and then make improvement reliable.

If you do not turn your constraints into strategic inputs that shape your success, they will become excuses that justify your failure.

— L. CHRISTINA-M. JACKSON

INTRODUCTION

Law school was not designed for people with full lives. It was built around assumptions: flexible schedules, minimal outside obligations, and uninterrupted focus, all of which do not reflect the realities many students face today. Legal education still operates on those assumptions. That is why students are told to treat law school like a full-time job. For many, that premise is simply not practical.

Even traditional students struggle under the volume and pace of law school. For non-traditional students, those balancing careers, families, caregiving responsibilities, financial pressure, or geographic instability, the challenge is not merely academic. It is structural.

If you are reading this book, you already understand that reality. You may be a second-career student. A parent. A caregiver. A professional working full-time. You may be older and carrying responsibilities that will not pause for midterms or finals. You may be operating under time scarcity, financial constraint, and emotional load that most law school guidance does not meaningfully address.

Yet here you are.
Because this degree serves a larger purpose.
Because failure is not an option.
Because the stakes are high, the investment is significant, and trial and error is an expensive way to learn in a system that measures performance from the very beginning.

What non-traditional students need is not more motivation, more grit, or more generic advice. What you need is a *strategic system* that works within the life you have. That is what this book attempts to provide.

I have encountered countless non-traditional law students who have started and completed law school despite significant adversity. The Constraint-Driven Method™ was developed under constraint, not ideal conditions. I began law school with two children under the age of two, welcomed another during my final year, navigated an overseas deployment during 1L, and relocated during 3L. I did not enter with a strong LSAT score, but I graduated magna cum laude. The difference was not circumstance, it was structure.

WHO THIS BOOK IS FOR

This book is written for students whose lives do not conform to the assumptions built into legal education but who are no less capable, committed, and ambitious.

In this book, "non-traditional" does not mean unprepared or disadvantaged. It means operating under real constraints that must be accounted for rather than ignored. Constraints are not failure-triggers. They are fixed variables. The mistake is trying to succeed as if they do not exist.

If You Are a Prospective Student

Law school is not about intelligence alone. It is a constrained performance environment. Your decision to attend should be based on a reasonable fit with your constraints, not on prestige or impulse.

If you are considering law school, understand this: admission is only the first hurdle in a demanding and sustained process.

Before enrolling, consider the following:

- Why you are drawn to the law

- Which school aligns with your interests and circumstances

- How you will complete the degree within your existing constraints

After you are admitted, your task changes so that it is no longer how to get into law school but how to perform once there. Law school evaluates how well you think, write, and perform under time pressure relative to others operating under similar conditions.

Before you commit, assess not only your interest in the law, but your capacity to operate within these constraints and your willingness to build systems that make that performance sustainable.

If You Are a 1L

Congratulations on clearing the hurdles of admission. You have studied for the LSAT, completed applications, and secured your place. Now the real work begins. As you begin your first semester, keep the following in mind:

- The adjustment period is real

- Systems matter more than effort

- Early positioning shapes your trajectory

The first year is the most volatile phase of law school. The rules are unfamiliar. Feedback is delayed. Grading is comparative.

This is not the time to rely on instinct alone. It is the time to build structure on how you read, outline, practice, and recover.

Early systems create stability, and stability drives performance. Your first exams will reveal whether your approach is working. Pay attention, adjust early, and refine your system with intention.

If You Are a 2L

You should take pride in completing the most demanding phase of law school. At this point, the risk is no longer confusion, it is misalignment. Opportunities will expand: you can now apply to join journals or organizations, get internships or certifications. But more options do not automatically improve outcomes. As you become more familiar with the system, beware of the following risks:

- Overcommitment

- The tradeoff between résumé-building and actual performance

- Misalignment with your goals

Performance does not come from accumulating achievements. It comes from aligning goals with specific successes. Every commitment should serve a defined objective. If it does not, it becomes a constraint that works against you.

If You Are in Your Final Year

Law school does not "end" per se; it transitions. In your final year, you must do the following:

- Plan for bar exam preparation

- Prepare for entrance into the profession

- Shift your focus to transfer of skills and performance

If you are in your final year, the question is no longer whether you can perform: it is whether your performance and skills are transferable and how to ensure they are.

The bar exam, employment decisions, and professional expectations will not reduce the constraints you are under. Rather, the constraints will change their form. Your objective now is not reinvention. It is consolidation. What works must be refined and carried forward.

Regardless of where you are, the principle remains the same: performance in law school is not accidental. It is designed, executed, and sustained under constraint.

Why Common Advice Fails

Much of the advice given to non-traditional law students is technically sound but practically incomplete. It assumes unlimited time, consistent energy, and the ability to reorganize one's entire life around school. When non-traditional students attempt to follow that advice and do not succeed, the result is often guilt, self-doubt, and unnecessary underperformance.

The problem is not effort. The problem is design.

Law school is an evaluative system governed by predictable structures: grading curves, professor expectations, institutional discretion, and timing-based feedback loops. Students who understand how this system operates, and who align accordingly, gain an advantage unrelated to intelligence or hours studied.

This book teaches you how to do exactly that.

At the core of this book is the Constraint-Driven Method™: a strategic performance framework built around the realities of your actual life, not ideal conditions.

Rather than asking:

"How does a law student succeed?"

the Method reframes the inquiry:

"Given your existing constraints, how can you optimize outcomes?"

It is built on five pillars, ten core principles, and three operational domains that work together to help non-traditional students

- preserve endurance without burnout

- execute efficiently under pressure

- leverage institutional systems ethically

- avoid preventable academic damage

- translate law school performance into long-term advantage

How This Book Is Organized

The chapters that follow are structured deliberately.

- Part I establishes what non-traditional law students must understand before classes begin.

- Parts II through IV apply the Method across internal endurance, performance execution, and relational & institutional leverage.

- Part V addresses sustaining performance alongside real-life responsibilities.

- Part VI focuses on outcomes and next moves, including how to carry the Method beyond law school.

- Part VII provides limited tools and templates for immediate application.

This book does not promise ease. Law school *is* demanding, as it should be. What this book promises instead is clarity. Clarity about how the system works, where effort produces the greatest return, and how to operate strategically when time, energy, and margin are limited. Practiced consistently, the principles in this book position you not merely to survive law school but to excel on your terms and within your constraints.

PART I — WHAT NON-TRADITIONAL LAW STUDENTS MUST KNOW

"It always seems impossible until it's done."
—Nelson Mandela

1

THERE IS A SIMPLE PATHWAY TO SUCCESS IN LAW SCHOOL

Success in law school is not a function of effort alone. It is the product of alignment between your life, the institutional system you are entering, and the strategies you must use to operate within it. Before learning how to execute, you must understand what you are actually up against.

1. EFFORT ALONE IS NEVER ENOUGH

Many capable adults enter law school believing that success is a matter of working hard, reading excessively, and managing time aggressively. When that approach fails, they often internalize the failure as personal.

This belief rests on the incomplete equation that more time and effort produce better results.

Law school does not necessarily reward effort in proportion to hours invested in wrestling with the material. It rewards performance as evaluated through specific institutional mechanisms such as exams, grading curves, professor preferences, etc.

Students who misunderstand this often do the following:

- over-read without strategic focus

- allocate time inefficiently

- mistake busyness for progress

- work harder while falling further behind

For non-traditional students, this mismatch is costly. Much of the advice given to non-traditional law students is not wrong. It just does not fully apply to them.

"Read everything."
"Brief everything."
"Join every organization."
"Treat law school like it's your full-time job."
"Network, network, network."

These recommendations rarely account for students whose lives already require full-time execution elsewhere.

When non-traditional students attempt to follow this advice and inevitably fall short, the result is often guilt, shame, or disengagement. The problem is framed as a failure of discipline rather than a failure of design.

This book rejects that framing because advice that ignores constraints is misleading.

2. NON-TRADITIONAL LAW STUDENTS NEED BETTER SYSTEMS

The central premise of this book is simple: *Non-traditional law students need better systems.*

A non-traditional law student is not defined by age, background, or identity. The term refers to students whose academic performance must coexist with sustained external responsibilities that law school does not account for. These responsibilities may include work, caregiving, parenting, health considerations, financial pressure, or other non-negotiable commitments.

In this book, a constraint refers to any fixed condition that limits time, energy, flexibility, or control and cannot be eliminated through effort alone. Constraints are not personal shortcomings or temporary inconveniences. They are structural realities that shape how performance must be designed.

When analyzed honestly and incorporated intentionally, constraints can become strategic inputs. In finance, liabilities are accounted for, not wished away. In operations, resource limits shape strategy. Law school is no different. Some constraints are permanent. Others are situational. All must be acknowledged. Constraints are fixed variables, not obstacles to be ignored.

A constraint is not inherently negative. In systems thinking, constraints define the parameters within which effective solutions must operate. Rather than attempting to eliminate these realities, successful students incorporate them into the structure of their study process. When deliberately integrated into a learning system, constraints become inputs that strengthen performance rather than weaken it.

Professional experience, for example, often develops habits directly transferable to law school performance. Work experience in managing deadlines, prioritizing competing demands, and executing work under pressure closely mirror the conditions of timed examinations and high-stakes academic assessments. When approached deliberately, these prior experiences provide a foundation for disciplined study and exam preparation.

Family responsibilities can function in a similar way. Explaining legal rules to others forces clarity of thought and exposes gaps in understanding. Verbalizing concepts aloud strengthens retention and sharpens analytical precision. Conversations that might otherwise appear to interrupt study time can become opportunities to rehearse reasoning and simplify complex ideas.

The key distinction lies in how these realities are framed. When treated as interruptions, professional and family responsibilities fragment attention and reduce available study time. When incorporated intentionally into a performance system, they become structured opportunities to reinforce learning.

The Constraint-Driven Method therefore does not ask non-traditional students to study as if these responsibilities did not exist. Instead, it teaches them to design systems that transform unavoidable constraints into productive inputs.

Practical Examples

Children, often the household's Chief Disturbing Officers, can unexpectedly become valuable learning partners. Explaining complex legal concepts in simple terms to children forces precision and reveals gaps in understanding.

A spouse can serve as an ever-present mock judge or opposing counsel, someone with whom to rehearse advocacy, explain legal rules aloud, and test the clarity of one's reasoning.

As mentioned above, professional experience in managing deadlines, prioritizing competing demands, and executing under pressure translates directly into disciplined performance during timed exams and high-stakes assessments. When used deliberately, it becomes leverage.

Traditional law school advice often assumes that students can reorganize their lives around institutional demands. For students operating under constraint, this assumption does not hold. When guidance ignores real operating conditions, it does not produce better performance. What it produces is inefficiency, fatigue, and avoidable failure.

This book does not offer motivation, platitudes, or abstract study tips. It provides a structured method that teaches students how to:

- identify where effort produces the highest return

- avoid predictable academic damage

- engage institutional resources strategically

- maintain endurance without burnout

- align execution with how outcomes are actually determined

Students operating with a greater margin may afford trial-and-error experimentation, late correction, and inefficient routines that eventually work. Non-traditional students cannot. When time or energy is wasted, there is little buffer to absorb the loss.

Better systems are not a preference. They are a requirement. Effective systems minimize decision fatigue, highlight meaningful signals, ensure consistent results, and remain reliable under pressure. Without systems, performance depends on limited willpower and endurance. Systems provide a sustainable alternative.

The Constraint-Driven Method™ exists because performance under constraint cannot depend on improvisation.

It must be engineered.

2

THE NON-TRADITIONAL LAW STUDENT READINESS ASSESSMENT

This assessment is for individual self-evaluation. *Institutional use, reproduction, or adaptation requires written permission.*

1. INSTRUCTIONS

Write "Yes," "No," or "I Don't Know" next to each question. Answer honestly. This is not a test of worth but rather it is a test of preparedness.

SECTION I: MOTIVATION & CLARITY

1) Do you have a clear reason for pursuing law school at this stage of your life that goes beyond prestige or income?

2) Can you articulate why you chose your law school institution, and what support they offer to non-traditional students?

3) Have you reflected on how law school will affect your family, work, or caregiving responsibilities?

4) Have you researched what law school life actually looks like for your circumstances on a daily basis?

5) Does pursuing law school advance your long-term objectives once personal, financial, and family constraints are fully accounted for?

SECTION II: PRACTICAL READINESS

1) Have you realistically assessed how much time you can dedicate weekly to law school work (reading load, class preparation, exams, etc.)?

2) Do you know your peak mental energy hours and how to protect them?

3) Have you identified non-negotiable obligations that will compete with law school?

4) Do you have a plan for childcare, elder care, or work coverage during high-pressure periods or life emergencies?

5) Have you identified any ethical, scheduling, or professional conflicts between your current career and legal education or practice?

SECTION III: ACADEMIC & INSTITUTIONAL AWARENESS

1) Do you understand law school grading approaches?

2) Are you familiar with law school exam formats?

3) Are you aware of the academic support resources available at your law school and online?

4) Do you have a law school mentor?

5) Have you committed to saying "no" to obligations that conflict with academic priorities?

SECTION IV: SUPPORT SYSTEMS

1)   Do you have at least one person who supports your decision to attend law school?

2)   Do you have available people who can help when law school demands peak?

3)   Have you set clearly defined boundaries in your current social circles to focus on law school?

4)   Do you have a written plan for academic collaboration?

5)   Do you know your institution point of contact for emergencies?

SECTION V: ENDURANCE & SELF-MANAGEMENT

1)   Have you done a recent health assessment?

2)   Have you adjusted your financial planning to capture law school costs?

3)   Do you have strategies for managing stress & exhaustion without self-destructing?

4)   Are you aware of your personal rest and recovery patterns and how they influence performance under pressure?

5)   Have you researched ways to overcome uncertainty, delayed feedback, and ambiguity?

2.   SCORING & INTERPRETATION

Count every "No" or "I Don't Know."

0–5

Strong Foundation This shows a high level of readiness. You are entering law school with awareness rather than illusion.

6–10

Moderate Readiness You likely are on the right track, but several gaps need attention preferably before you start class.

11–15

High Risk Without Adjustment Law school is possible, but proceeding without deliberate planning increases the likelihood of burnout, underperformance, or unnecessary stress.

16 or More

Pause and Reassess Entering law school without addressing some areas will place an unfair burden on yourself and those who depend on you.

This assessment is not a measure of intelligence or potential. It is a diagnostic tool designed to (1) identify constraints that interfere with performance and (2) guide you toward the appropriate corrective strategy.

3

LAW SCHOOL IS TRIPARTITE

Law school is often treated as a single event: a three-year tunnel to be endured and exited. In reality, this framing is incomplete. Law school is tripartite:

- Before law school

- During law school

- After law school

Each phase imposes different demands. Preparation that ignores any one of them is structurally weak. Success does not come from surviving the middle part alone. It comes from designing for and overcoming *all three phases*.

---

1. BEFORE LAW SCHOOL: PREPARATION AND POSITIONING

The most misunderstood phase of law school is the one that occurs before the first day of class.

At this stage, non-traditional students are often pulled between two unhelpful extremes: rushing in unprepared or postponing indefinitely while waiting for ideal conditions that may never arrive. Neither approach is strategic. The objective is not certainty or comfort. It is *informed readiness* based on your *actual circumstances*.

Preparation Is More Than Admission

For many students, preparation for law school is treated as synonymous with gaining admission. The Law School Admission Test (LSAT), application essays, letters of recommendation, and scholarships consume attention. Once the admission offer arrives, preparation is assumed to be complete.

This is a mistake.

Admission determines *access*. It does not determine *performance*.

It is common to hear a progression of frustrations at each stage of the legal path: law students often say the LSAT did not prepare them for law school; graduates remark that law school did not prepare them for the bar exam; and new attorneys observe that the bar exam did not prepare them for legal practice.

That is because the skills, systems, and expectations required to enter each stage are different from those required to succeed within each phase. Preparing only for admission leaves students underprepared for the environment that awaits them.

From a tactical standpoint, the LSAT and admissions process measure aptitude and grit under *pre*–law school conditions. It is backward-looking. Law school, by contrast, measures execution within its own institutional mechanics. Therefore, success in the admission process does *not* guarantee success in law school itself.

Be forward-thinking. Prepare beyond LSAT performance and acceptance letters. Understand how law school actually operates, how performance is evaluated, and how your real life will interact with those demands once classes begin.

The purpose of the *before law school* phase is not merely to get in. It is to enter *positioned to perform*.

This phase includes:

- Selecting an institution with realistic alignment between your goals, constraints, and the institution's academic and career support

- Setting realistic expectations about time, energy, emotional load, and early performance

- Understanding law school performance metrics (exam formats, grading curves, professor discretion)

- Planning for and communicating with family, employers, and key people who will be affected by the demands of law school on you

- Gaining a baseline familiarity with legal materials (not mastering doctrine)

- Pre-designing study, scheduling, and recovery systems that can operate under your actual circumstances

- Treating orientation as part of the academic term, not an administrative formality

Students who neglect this preparation spend their first semester reacting instead of executing. And the cost of that delay becomes evident quickly.

Readiness Is Not Perfection

Readiness means accounting for disruption without assuming collapse. The objective is not to prevent adversity, but to build systems with enough margin, support, and flexibility to endure it.

Preparation will not eliminate uncertainty because even the most thoughtful plans are vulnerable to disruption.

Serious illness, injury, miscarriage, divorce, forced relocation, layoff, or family loss can unfortunately occur during law school regardless of preparation. These events are realities of life. The way to overcome them is to operate under systems that can bend without breaking.

Practical Pre-Entry Steps

Before classes officially begin:

- Attend a pre-1L summer program to the extent possible

- Research and review materials that prior students and law professors find useful at the outset

- Reach out to alumni or faculty and ask for practical advice

- As soon as schedules and syllabi are released, obtain your materials and start reading

Many schools have a "Week Zero" filled with orientations and administrative tasks. Treat this period as part of the academic term, not a soft opening. Early traction reduces friction later.

Law school places you in competition with exceptionally capable peers, some of whom arrive with strong familiarity with legal materials and expectations. Entering this environment without having read a judicial opinion, knowing how to brief a case, or being able to define a tort creates unnecessary shock and stress.

Law school cohorts routinely include:

- *Paralegals*

- *former teachers*

- *engineers*

- *military personnel*

- *healthcare professionals*

- *scientists*

- *finance professionals*

- *entrepreneurs*

- *public servants*

all of whom bring different forms of training, discipline, and exposure to structured thinking.

The issue is not where you begin. It is whether you can develop a system quickly enough to close the gap.

2.   DURING LAW SCHOOL: EXECUTION

This phase receives the most attention because it is where performance is evaluated, grades are earned, and stress concentrates.

Students who struggle during this phase often confuse effort with strategy. They work hard without alignment. They study in the abstract, overlook evaluators, resist institutional norms, or overextend themselves through guilt-driven overwork. They let busy work become a substitute for effective work.

Execution under constraint requires something different:

- constraint-aware systems

- early feedback loops

- clarity about how exams are graded

- relational and institutional leverage

- strategic rest

Law school is not overcome through blind intensity. You must navigate it through sustained, targeted execution. This is where the application of the Constraint-Driven Method™ is most visible. Through steady application, its principles begin to shape how you structure your time, attention, and effort.

3.   AFTER LAW SCHOOL: TRANSFER, NOT RELIEF

This phase is often the most neglected, albeit one of the most consequential. Many students experience graduation as a finish line. In reality, it is a transition. The structure of law school may disappear, but the demands of the profession remain.

The period immediately following law school typically includes:

- bar preparation

- entry into legal practice or JD-preferred roles

- development of professional identity

- long-term endurance in high-pressure environments

Students who approach law school as an isolated academic event often overlook the importance of building durable skills and professional relationships. As a result, the transition after graduation can feel disorienting.

Legal knowledge evolves quickly as doctrine, institutions, and social conditions change. Skills, professional judgment, and relationships, however, remain transferable across roles and over time. So, as you navigate law school, remember that today's peers are tomorrow's colleagues and today's deliverables are tomorrow's professional reputation.

Additionally, you must have an exit strategy, whether it is preparing to study for the bar or starting a judicial clerkship immediately after graduation. The plan does not need to be rigid, but it should exist. Preparation for the post-law-school phase should not be postponed until after graduation. Delaying this planning can slow your ability to position yourself to use your law degree effectively and move forward with purpose in the profession.

For this reason, the Constraint-Driven Method™ is designed to extend beyond the classroom. A method that functions only within the academic setting is too limited to support the realities of a legal career.

4. WHY PREPARATION MUST SPAN ALL THREE PHASES

Preparation must span all three phases because each phase feeds the next:

- poor preparation before law school increases stress during law school

- dysfunctional habits during law school carry forward after graduation

- lack of vision for after law school distorts priorities during law school

Law school is not just about becoming a law student. It is about becoming a legal professional.

When you understand that law school is tripartite, you stop rushing, you stop panicking, and you stop treating setbacks as failures. Instead, you begin sequencing correctly.

Preparation becomes intentional.
Pressure becomes manageable.
Outcomes become durable.

Law school is not something you simply get through. It is a commitment you must be prepared for, operate within strategically, and be equipped to build upon after you leave.

4

Common Constraints Non-Traditional Law Students Encounter

Most students struggle at first because they enter law school with assumptions shaped by prior success in systems that reward different behaviors. What they lack initially is not discipline or capability, but accurate information about adjusting to the law school environment.

1. Rookie Mistakes: What Not to Do in Law School

The first constraints students encounter in law school are predictable gaps between effort and evaluation that eventually lead to the following common mistakes:

- Ignoring law school's tripartite structure

- Spending the first semester self-calibrating in the dark

- Overvaluing prior professional or academic success

- Studying for broad understanding instead of evaluation

- Reading every case from the beginning to the end literally

- Assuming that effort outside of graded assessments will be rewarded

- Preparing generically for professor-specific exams

- Using peers as the primary measure of progress

- Expecting uniform excellence across all subjects

- Not having a reasonable plan for success

- Waiting for failure before adopting or adjusting a performance strategy

- Trying to navigate law school alone

- Discounting incremental improvement

- Giving up too early

These mistakes are not signs that law school is beyond reach. They reflect an incomplete understanding of how the system operates.

2. YOU MUST EXPECT AN ADJUSTMENT PERIOD

The adjustment period is not uniform. It is shaped by the constraints each student carries into law school. While no two students are identical, most non-traditional students operate within one or more of the following profiles. These are not identities but conditions to recognize and plan around.

FIVE COMMON NON-TRADITIONAL PROFILES

The descriptions that follow are observed patterns across non-traditional law students. However, they do not capture every individual circumstance or variation within each profile.

Their purpose is directional: to provide a broad, experience-based view of how different constraints tend to shape a semester, where risks commonly emerge, and how performance can be structured in response.

The Working Professional

Working professionals are students who maintain part-time or full-time employment alongside their coursework; they often operate within fixed work schedules that limit available study time and reduce flexibility during the academic week. Working professionals fall into two broad categories: those who need a Juris Doctorate to advance within their current field (often in compliance-driven roles) and those who will be using their law degree to transition into a new career path.

Constraint Reality: Working professionals operate within fixed work schedules that restrict available study time and carry cognitive fatigue into academic work.

Primary Risk: Fragmented attention and chronic fatigue.

What the Semester Looks Like: Weeks are pre-committed before they begin. Class time is fixed. Work obligations are non-negotiable. Study time exists in narrow, predefined blocks like early mornings, late evenings, and weekends. There is little margin for recovery if a week is lost.

Common Pitfalls:

- Attempting to study reactively rather than on a fixed schedule

- Underestimating cognitive fatigue after work hours

- Sacrificing sleep to "catch up," resulting in diminishing returns

- Treating available time as sufficient without structuring how it is used

Strengths:

- Existing discipline and time accountability

- Professional communication skills

- Familiarity with operating under external expectations

What to Expect: You will have very limited time. You will not be able to recover easily from disorganization. Progress will depend on whether your limited hours are used with precision.

Operational Implication: Performance must be engineered with precision. Study time cannot be extended at will as it must be protected, structured, and used deliberately. Study blocks should be pre-assigned and tied to specific outputs, with work executed in limited, high-efficiency windows.

The Career Changer

Career changers are students transitioning from prior professions, often after time away from academic environments; they may enter law school with established work habits that do not fully align with the demands of legal study.

Constraint Reality: Career changers have limited familiarity with academic evaluation structures, often expending significant effort inefficiently until they identify what actually drives performance.

Primary Risk: They may have misalignment between prior success strategies and law school expectations.

What the Semester Looks Like: Early weeks may feel deceptively manageable. Reading is completed, notes are taken, and effort is high, but results do not always reflect that effort. Feedback, when it comes, may not align with expectations built from prior professional success.

Common Pitfalls:

- Relying on familiar methods that do not translate to legal analysis

- Overvaluing effort without verifying output quality

- Delaying practice exams and application-based learning

- Assuming prior achievement will carry forward without adjustment

Strengths:

- Work ethic and accountability

- Ability to manage long-term goals

- Real-world context that can deepen understanding

What to Expect: Career changers may need to relearn how to learn. Performance will depend on how quickly they adapt to law school's specific demands: issue-spotting, structured analysis, and time-bound writing.

Operational Implication: Prior experience is an asset only if adapted. Law school rewards a specific form of analysis and communication that must be learned deliberately.

The Caregiver

Caregivers are students responsible for children, family members, or other dependents.

Constraint Reality: Caregivers often operate within unpredictable and interrupted schedules shaped by non-negotiable responsibilities. These responsibilities limit uninterrupted study time.

Primary Risk: Unpredictable disruptions and divided cognitive load.

What the Semester Looks Like: Even well-structured plans are interrupted. Study sessions are shortened, delayed, or fragmented. Attention is divided between academic demands and real-time responsibilities that cannot be deferred.

Common Pitfalls:

- Expecting uninterrupted study conditions

- Measuring productivity by duration rather than completion

- Carrying guilt that erodes focus during available study time

- Restarting inefficiently after interruptions

Strengths:

- High tolerance for responsibility and pressure

- Strong prioritization instincts

- Emotional resilience under sustained demand

What to Expect: The caregiver's schedule will not be fully controllable. Some days will not go as planned. Progress will depend on how quickly and effectively they can re-enter focused work.

Operational Implication: Consistency will not come from control over time, but from systems that absorb interruption and allow rapid re-entry into focused work.

The First-Generation Law Student

First-generation or unfamiliar-with-the-system students are those with limited exposure to the norms of law school.

International students sometimes fall within this category as they must overcome language and cultural barriers that affect how legal education is delivered and evaluated.

Constraint Reality: Limited exposure to legal education norms, expectations, and informal knowledge networks, often accompanied by uncertainty, self-doubt, and heightened vulnerability to imposter syndrome.

Primary Risk: Operating without access to unwritten rules and strategic guidance.

What the Semester Looks Like: Much of what others seem to understand implicitly must be learned explicitly. There may be uncertainty about how to outline, how to study, how exams are graded, or what actually matters.

Common Pitfalls:

- Spending time on tasks that are not performance-relevant

- Delaying questions due to uncertainty or hesitation

- Misinterpreting silence or lack of clarity as personal deficiency

- Operating in isolation instead of seeking structured guidance

Strengths:

- Willingness to work and persist

- Openness to structured systems

- Ability to adopt effective methods without needing to unlearn habits

What to Expect: There will be information gaps early. Progress will depend on how quickly those gaps are identified and closed.

Operational Implication: Information gaps must be closed proactively. What others absorb informally must be sought out intentionally and early.

The Hybrid Student

Hybrid students are generally geographically or structurally constrained; they may commute long distances, participate in asynchronous programs, or otherwise operate with reduced access to in-person integration within the law school environment.

Constraint Reality: Hybrid students experience reduced access to in-person interaction, informal learning, and institutional visibility.

Primary Risk: Isolation from key information flows and missed opportunities for leverage. Some guest lectures and courses are limited to students who attend primarily in person, and not all professors are comfortable with the online format or equipped to engage fully in a virtual setting.

What the Semester Looks Like: Engagement is largely self-directed. Class participation may be mediated through screens and online work. Informal conversations before class, after class, and in hallways are limited or absent. Access to peers and professors requires intentional effort.

Common Pitfalls:

- Treating physical distance as a reason for reduced engagement

- Missing informal but critical information shared among peers

- Delaying outreach to professors or support services

- Remaining invisible within the institution

Strengths:

- Flexibility in managing time and environment

- Reduced commuting and logistical friction

- Greater control over study conditions

What to Expect: Opportunities will not present themselves passively. Access, visibility, and connection must be created deliberately.

Operational Implication: Engagement must be deliberate. Visibility, relationships, and access will not occur passively. They must be constructed.

Many students operate within more than one of these profiles simultaneously. The purpose of identifying these constraints is not to discourage you but to alert you to what realistically awaits you.

Law school does not adjust its expectations to match these conditions. The Method exists to help meet those expectations anyway. For students who do not actively account for their constraints in designing their performance approach, or who downplay their reality, early outcomes often fail to reflect the level of effort invested.

THE FIRST EXAM REALITY CHECK

For many students, the first graded law school exams are shockingly disappointing. This experience is common. It is not a sign that something has gone wrong.

Law school grading is unfamiliar, delayed, and comparative. It does not reward effort per se, prior success, or professional competence in the way many students are used to. Early results often reflect misalignment, *not* inability.

I am telling you this now so that when it happens, you recognize it for what it is. Nothing strange is happening. You are not failing. You are learning a new evaluative system.

Why the First Results Often Disappoint

Early assessments frequently reveal:

- unfamiliar grading criteria

- differences between understanding material and *applying* it under exam conditions

- a mismatch between preparation style and evaluation method

These gaps are expected. They are part of the transition, not a judgment on your capacity to succeed.

Do Not Let Surprise Become Self-Doubt

The greatest risk is not a disappointing grade. It is the meaning students assign to it. Without proper context and understanding, students conclude:
"I'm not cut out for this."
"I'm behind everyone else."
"I made a mistake coming here."

These conclusions are so premature and often wrong.

Understanding that early results are often disappointing does not make them irrelevant. On the contrary, it makes them usable. They become information, *not* identity. This awareness allows you to:

- respond strategically rather than emotionally

- seek clarification without shame

- adjust strategies before damage accumulates

Do not let your confidence collapse simply because the adjustment period looks like disappointment. Law school is a system. Systems *can* be learned.

Do Not Let Outliers Shake You

Every law school has its share of *outliers*.

Outliers are students who appear to master the system quickly and perform far ahead of the curve. Some maintain near-perfect academic records or progress through the curriculum at an accelerated pace. Their performance is genuine, but their circumstances are rarely representative of the broader student population.

Many enter with unusually strong analytical training, fewer competing obligations, exceptional test-taking instincts or training, or prior exposure to legal reasoning. Modeling study habits after outliers is gambling the sure path for the rare trajectory because exceptional outcomes can emerge from conditions that are not visible and are difficult to replicate. That is why you should not let outliers shake your confidence or lose yourself in wanting to mimic their rare trajectories.

Tailor your approach to your own reality so you can stay consistent.

5

THE CONSTRAINT-DRIVEN METHOD™ EXPLAINED

The Constraint-Driven Method™ is a way of operating in high-stakes environments by designing performance accounting for everyday life as it exists; rather than around idealized conditions that rarely apply. Most professional and academic guidance assumes that success requires reorganizing one's life around the demands of law school. For non-traditional students, this is clearly unrealistic and often counterproductive.

The Constraint-Driven Method™ begins from a different starting point. It does not ask how a law student should *ideally* succeed. It asks how performance can be *maximized* given the student's *actual* conditions. The Method does not seek to eliminate these conditions. It designs performance systems that account for them honestly.

---

1.   THE ARCHITECTURE OF THE METHOD

The Constraint-Driven Method™ operates through four sequential steps that determine how performance systems succeed or fail under constraint.

This is the blueprint: (1) Recognition—identifying your limits, (2) Signal Identification—focusing on what drives high performance, (3) System Design—building a routine around your realities, and (4) Sustainability and Transfer—making your performance design last.

Step One is Recognition

This step is an honest identification of non-negotiable limitations that may be fixed or not. They should be treated as design inputs, not obstacles.

Practical Example: A working parent who is in law school wants top grades. Instead of pretending they can study eight hours a day, they recognize they only have three focused hours each evening after their children go to sleep. That becomes the design constraint. Rather than trying to adhere to an imaginary ideal of eight hours of study, which simply is not possible for this student, the system is built around the three focused hours.

Step Two is Signal Identification

This step is the ability to distinguish what actually drives evaluation and outcomes from activity that feels productive but carries little weight.

Practical Example: A student spends hours highlighting textbooks and attending every optional workshop. But grades are determined almost entirely by one final exam. The real signal is mastering how professors test. Once that is clear, effort shifts toward exam practice, not passive reading.

Step Three is System Design

This step is the ability to create structure. You must organize time, effort, and priorities so performance does not depend on mood, motivation, or perfect conditions. You remove reliance on willpower and replace it with routine.

Practical Example: Instead of deciding each night what to study, a student creates a fixed weekly structure:
>Monday: Update outlines

> Tuesday: Rule memorization
> Wednesday: Practice exam questions alone
> Thursday: Rule reinforcement
> Friday: Timed exam drills and issue spotting
> Saturday: Practice exam questions with study group
> Sunday: Reading assignments

The decision-making is done once so execution becomes automatic.

Step Four is Sustainability and Transfer

This step is about ensuring the system holds under fatigue, disruption, and competing demands, and can be used beyond a single semester or context. If it only works when you feel energized and focused, it is fragile.

Practical Example: A student working part-time begins the final month of the semester when their work schedule unexpectedly increases for several weeks. Instead of attempting to maintain the same study volume, the student adjusts the system. Lower-priority activities such as extensive case rereading are reduced, while the most consequential work (practice exams, rule synthesis, and issue spotting) is protected. The total hours decline, but the core study signals remain intact, allowing the student to continue progressing without losing direction.
Later, the same structure proves useful during bar preparation and in professional practice, where competing responsibilities and limited time similarly require protecting the most important work while allowing other tasks to adjust.

This blueprint teaches non-traditional students how to perform well without pretending. It forces clarity first. Then prioritization. Then structure. Then durability. These steps are not just tactics. They are the order of operations for designing reliable performance. Skipping a layer produces predictable breakdown. Completing them in sequence produces stability under pressure.

What the Method Is—and Is Not

The Constraint-Driven Method™ is a performance design framework. It is not a motivational philosophy, a therapeutic intervention, or an advocacy tool.

It does not promise ease, balance, or comfort. It does not remove institutional demands or eliminate hardship. It does not function by lowering standards.

Instead, the Method provides a structured way to design performance systems that operate reliably within real-world constraints. It treats law school as an institutional environment governed by predictable incentives and patterns, and it teaches deliberate engagement with those conditions.

The Method assumes capability. It is not remediation. It is not counseling. It does not address emotional processing beyond what is necessary for operational stability. It is not a substitute for accommodations, support services, or professional care where those are appropriate.

Its purpose is more precise: to help individuals convert effort into outcomes when margin is limited.

Understanding what the Method does *not* attempt to do is essential to using it correctly.

A Working Model: The Limited-Block Tower

Now, imagine being asked to build a tower.

You are given a limited number of blocks.
The ground is unstable.
The conditions will not improve.

There are no instructions

How will you build your tower?

Most people respond by stacking the pieces straight up, fast, and high. But since the floor is unstable, stacking faster does not prevent the tower from falling.

The failure is not about intelligence. It is not about discipline. It is about *design*.

Working harder does not make up for poor planning. Success in this scenario is not about height. It is about stability. Any tower with a larger base that stands is stronger than the tallest tower that collapses.

The Constraint-Driven Method™ applies this same logic to law school.

As a non-traditional student, you must:

- begin by accepting your constraints as design inputs
- build carefully
- prioritize the pieces that matter most
- design for *pressure*, not perfection

The goal is to build a structure that holds.

2.   THE FIVE PILLARS

The Constraint-Driven Method™ rests on five structural pillars. Each pillar addresses a distinct operational requirement. When one pillar is weak or missing, performance becomes unstable. When all five are present and aligned, performance becomes durable, even under sustained pressure.

PILLAR ONE: CONSTRAINT ANALYSIS

Constraint Analysis is the point of entry into the Method. Before strategies are designed or goals are set, reality must be assessed honestly.

This pillar requires a clear inventory of the conditions under which performance must occur, including (but not limited to):

- available time

- energy cycles

- family and work obligations

- non-negotiables

- foreseeable risk points

Most students design schedules around aspiration.
Constraint-driven students must design systems around realistic execution. The objective is not maximum effort. It is maximum *return on effort.*

PILLAR TWO: SELECTIVE MASTERY

Selective Mastery governs where limited resources are applied. Because time and energy are finite, they must be directed toward material that reliably produces evaluative return. This pillar requires identifying and mastering what actually matters:

- high-yield tasks

- frequently tested issues

- professor-specific priorities

- strategies that meaningfully affect grades

Law school does not reward equal attention to all material. It rewards depth where it matters most. Selective Mastery disciplines attention so effort is invested where it produces results.

PILLAR THREE: OUTCOME-DRIVEN DISCIPLINE

Outcome-driven discipline governs how effort is converted into results. It replaces activity-based validation with results-based judgment. It shifts the central question from:

"Am I working hard enough?" to

"Is my effort producing the outcomes this course actually rewards?"

This pillar requires testing every activity against two criteria: whether it (1) improves performance in graded formats, or (2) advances defined career objectives. If it does neither, it should be set aside without guilt.

PILLAR FOUR: CONSISTENT RHYTHMS

Consistent Rhythms are the stabilizing force of the Method. A rhythm is a repeatable pattern of execution designed to function within real constraints. It does not require perfect days or uninterrupted weeks; it assumes imperfection and continues forward regardless.

Performance under constraint is sustained by *consistency*, not intensity. Systems built on intensity require ideal conditions to function. Systems built on rhythm assume disruption and remain operational anyway.

The performance metric is *momentum*, not volume. Functional daily, weekly, monthly, and semester-long rhythms ensure progress continues even when time is scarce.

PILLAR FIVE: INSTITUTIONAL LEVERAGE

Institutional leverage begins with understanding the environment.

Law school operates through formal policies, informal norms, and discretionary decision-making. Ignoring this reality does not neutralize its effects; it simply places you at a disadvantage.

Constraint-driven students learn how the institution functions so they can navigate it intentionally rather than reactively by:

- engaging professors strategically

- interpreting grading structures accurately

- communicating professionally

- positioning themselves ethically within institutional boundaries

This pillar teaches informed participation in a system that rewards those who understand how it operates.

3.   THE TEN CORE PRINCIPLES

Where the five pillars define the Method, the core principles govern its use. They address predictable pressure points in the law school experience. They are:

- *Know Your Why* establishes a decision filter that anchors priorities before pressure distorts judgment.

- *Remember Your Why* restores continuity and direction after setbacks, fatigue, or performance dips.

- *Sleep Before You Quit* prevents exhaustion-driven decisions that lead capable students to exit prematurely.

- *Stay Ahead, Not Caught Up* creates buffer, so predictable friction does not compound into academic damage.

- *Seek Help Before You Need It* uses support as leverage early, when guidance is most effective and least costly.

- *Filter Out Noise* preserves efficiency by prioritizing authoritative feedback over peer speculation.

- *Repeat What Works for You* builds consistency by refining proven strategies instead of constantly reinventing.

- *Study and Emulate Success Where You Are* aligns effort with locally rewarded behaviors rather than generic study advice.

- *Build Your Law School Village* creates academic and emotional infrastructure in the form of community, such as classmates, colleagues, and friends, and this reduces isolation and burnout.

- *Know Your Institutional Gatekeepers* ensures you understand who controls key academic decisions and how to navigate discretion, policy, and flexibility before the stakes are high.

The ten core principles do not operate in isolation or in a fixed order. They are applied repeatedly as conditions change—during strong weeks, setbacks, or periods of fatigue.

Their effectiveness depends on *where* in the law school journey they are being applied. Some principles preserve endurance. Others govern execution. Others create leverage within the institution. For that reason, the Method organizes application into three operational domains.

4. THE THREE OPERATIONAL DOMAINS

While the core principles govern how decisions are made under constraint, the operational domains determine where those decisions are applied.

DOMAIN ONE: INTERNAL ENDURANCE—HOW YOU STAY IN LAW SCHOOL EVEN WHEN QUITTING FEELS RATIONAL

This domain addresses the psychological and physiological foundations that make persistence possible. Without endurance, no strategy, however well designed, can be executed. Endurance defines the limits of sustained performance.

Know Your Why. Do not consider the reason you decided to get a law degree as motivation only; it is also risk management. Your "why" must function as a decision filter, a prioritization tool, and an anchor when performance dips.

Remember Your Why. Endurance requires continuity. High-performing students revisit their purpose regularly and especially after setbacks, during personal crises, and near finals.

Sleep Before You Quit. Exhaustion distorts judgment. Resting is a strategic intervention that preserves cognitive bandwidth, regulates emotion, and prevents premature exit from law school.

DOMAIN TWO: PERFORMANCE EXECUTION—HOW RESULTS ARE PRODUCED AND SUSTAINED

This domain governs focus, effort allocation, and improvement. It is where strategy is executed.

Stay Ahead, Not Caught Up. Anticipation creates margin. You must foresee and address predictable friction points to avoid academic damage.

Seek Help Before You Need It. Asking questions early saves you trouble later. Instead of waiting to make a mistake to seek corrective measures, be proactive and learn from the experience or advice of others.

Filter Out Noise. It is better to prioritize authoritative feedback to preserve efficiency and alignment.

Repeat What Works for You. Sustained performance is built through disciplined repetition. Once a strategy produces results, refine it; do not replace it.

DOMAIN THREE: RELATIONAL & INSTITUTIONAL LEVERAGE— WHO AND WHAT HELPS YOU SUCCEED WITHIN THE SYSTEM

This domain addresses the people, structures, and informal power dynamics that shape outcomes in law school.

Study and Emulate Success Where You Are. Law schools are idiosyncratic systems. Success leaves clues. Researching success stories within your specific institution and copying systems that worked before, will decrease the odds of underperforming. However, you must adjust them to your own circumstances.

Build Your Law School Village. Non-traditional students should not operate alone. Academic and emotional support are necessary infrastructure, not extras. Burnout is often isolation in disguise. Find the right people with whom you can navigate law school. It makes a difference.

Know Your Institutional Gatekeepers. It is important to know who controls flexibility, accommodations, and policy. It will save you time when you need it.

The domains are sequential for a reason.

- Endurance enables execution
- Execution produces results
- Leverage amplifies outcomes

Each domain depends on the one before it. Without endurance, execution is inconsistent; without execution, there is nothing to leverage. If you break the sequence, performance is likely to become unstable.

5.   THE LOGIC OF PERFORMANCE UNDER CONSTRAINT

Performance under constraint reframes failure. For many non-traditional students, breakdown does not occur because of laziness or lack of intelligence. It occurs because stabilization, capacity, or alignment has been compromised. When constraints are ignored, performance fails for structural reasons, not personal ones.

When non-traditional students struggle in law school, it is often because they are attempting to perform within unstable or misaligned operating conditions. Sustainable performance begins by restoring operating conditions, not by demanding more output from an already strained system.

This model can be visualized as a pyramid that is hierarchical, not linear. You do not climb it once and remain at the top. You cycle through it as circumstances change such as when new responsibilities emerge, energy fluctuates, or pressure intensifies.

Level I: Stabilization — *Survival Before Strategy*
This level governs basic functioning. When sleep, emotional regulation, or predictability are unstable, judgment, focus, and retention deteriorate. No strategic effort can compensate for their absence. Without stabilization, higher-level effort is inefficient and fragile.

Level II: Capacity — *Energy, Time, and Cognitive Bandwidth*
This level governs how much effort can be absorbed productively. When time, energy, or cognitive bandwidth are exceeded, systems break down regardless of motivation or intent. Systems must fit reality, not aspiration.

Level III: Alignment — *Making Effort Sustainable*
This level governs sustainability. When students understand how law school actually evaluates performance, effort becomes targeted and coherent. Purpose aligns with mechanics.
Without alignment, students work harder but not strategically. Pressure increases while progress stalls.

Level IV: Execution — *Performance Under Constraint*
This level governs output. When lower-level conditions are stable, effort converts into measurable results. When they are unstable, execution becomes inconsistent, inefficient, and difficult to sustain. Execution does not create stability; it depends on it.

Level V: Leverage — *Expanding Outcomes*
Once execution is stabilized, relational and institutional leverage expand outcomes without additional effort.

This hierarchy clarifies a central principle of the Method: You do not demand peak performance from an unstable foundation. You restore the foundation first.

OPERATIONAL SUMMARY: PART I

This part requires you to abandon the assumption that effort alone produces results in law school. You must accept that non-traditional circumstances change how performance must be designed, not whether performance is possible.

You are expected to assess your readiness honestly, identify predictable friction points, and understand the institutional structure you are entering. This is not just a reflective exercise. It is a positioning exercise.

Before moving forward, you should have a clear understanding of your constraints, the common mistakes to avoid, and the logic of the Constraint-Driven Method™ as an operating framework.

PART II — INTERNAL ENDURANCE

"If you're walking down the right path and you're willing to keep walking, eventually you'll make progress." — **Barack Obama**

6

KNOW YOUR WHY

Without a clear sense of purpose, priorities blur, tradeoffs feel arbitrary, and pressure becomes unsustainable. Knowing why you seek a law degree is not about motivation; it is about anchoring and sustaining you on the path to your destination. This is what makes decision-making possible when conditions deteriorate.

---

1.   PURPOSE AS A STRATEGIC ASSET

Most law students treat their "why" as a motivational exercise, something articulated in a personal statement or recalled when coursework feels overwhelming.

In that framing, purpose is only emotional fuel: useful when energy is low. However, this framing misunderstands what a "why" actually does, particularly for non-traditional students.

Students carrying full lives do not enter law school casually. It is entered at a steep cost. The need for a functional "why" is not aspirational. It answers a harder question: *Why is this disruption justified?*

There will be times when law school collides with grief, exhaustion, illness, financial strain, or family instability. In those moments, ambition alone will be insufficient. Persistence will not be sustained by interest or prestige, but by a reason strong enough to justify continuing despite escalating costs.

A Well-Defined "Why" Functions as a Decision-Making Tool

For non-traditional students, a well-defined "why" performs three critical functions:

It narrows focus. When time and energy are limited, purpose determines what receives attention and what does not. A clear "why" filters distractions and prevents over-investment in activities that do not materially advance the end goal.

It stabilizes identity under pressure. Law school has a way of reducing students' self-worth to rankings, curves, and comparisons. A strong "why" anchors identity outside these institutional metrics.

It prevents premature exit. Many students leave law school not because they lack ability, but because the cost begins to feel unjustified. A clear "why" supplies meaning when feedback is delayed, effort is invisible, and progress feels ambiguous.

Knowing your "why" before law school and returning to it during moments of strain create coherence between intention and execution. Motivation fluctuates; purpose endures.

Your "Why" Must Survive Discomfort

Discomfort is not an anomaly in law school. It is a constant. Students experience discomfort when they:

- miss family time
- underperform despite sustained effort
- feel out of place among peers with fewer external obligations

- perform poorly in comparison to peers with similar or more external obligations
- confront gaps between the law's stated ideals and its real-world operation

A "why" rooted in convenience, prestige, or vague interest will fail under sustained pressure. A functional "why" must be emotionally grounded, morally coherent, and resilient under disappointment. It does not need to be dramatic. It needs to be durable and specific enough to withstand fatigue, frustration, and disillusionment.

Practical Example:
A general motivation such as "*I want to be a voice for the voiceless*" may feel inspiring, but it often lacks the precision needed to sustain effort when law school becomes frustrating or overwhelming.

By contrast, a motivation rooted in a concrete injustice such as "*I want to become the first female counsel in my rural community so that what happened to Mrs. X's children, who were severely harmed and never received justice, cannot happen again*" is far more likely to endure.

When the work becomes difficult, clarity about *why* you started makes persistence possible.

2.   HOW TO IDENTIFY A FUNCTIONAL WHY

Your "why" does not need to mirror anyone else's out there but it does need to meet a certain standard. A functional "why" should be able to answer the following questions:

- What injustice, gap, or responsibility do I feel compelled to address?

- Why does this matter *to me*, not abstractly?

- Would this still matter if recognition never came?

- Does this justify the sacrifices I am making right now?

- Why law, and not something adjacent or completely different?

- Why now?

- What responsibility do I feel prepared to carry when I succeed?

- What would quitting mean?

These are not philosophical questions. They are operational ones. Your answers will determine how you study, how you prioritize, and how you respond when law school tests your limits. If you cannot answer these questions clearly, your "why" is perhaps underdeveloped.

When your "why" is clear, effort becomes intentional because you are not reacting emotionally to each challenge. You are executing with intention.

You are no longer trying to keep up.
You are operating with direction.
You must define your "why" precisely enough to carry you through law school and beyond.

This principle strengthens the Constraint-Driven Method™ by anchoring execution rhythms in purpose rather than emotion.

7

REMEMBER YOUR WHY

Knowing your why is only the beginning. The more difficult task is remembering it once law school begins to erode clarity.

Law school has a unique way of narrowing your field of vision. What begins as a purpose-driven decision gradually becomes a sequence of tasks: reading, class preparation, outlines, exams, grades, repeat. Over time, the original reason you entered law school can feel distant, abstract, or irrelevant to the day-to-day grind.

When your life already contains competing demands, law school pressure does not simply exhaust you, it can displace meaning. You must not let your "why" fade away or get buried.

---

1.   REMEMBERING YOUR WHY REQUIRES DELIBERATE ACTION

Law school will test whether the cost *remains justified*. That tends to surface at predictable moments:

- after disappointing grades

- during finals, when exhaustion distorts judgment

- when family obligations collide with academic demands

- when legal outcomes feel misaligned with moral expectations

In those moments, the question is not whether the work is difficult. It is whether the effort is warranted. Many students assume that once purpose is identified, it will sustain them automatically. It will not.

Remembering your "why" is the act of regularly reconnecting present effort to original intention. This is not an exercise in affirmation. It is the preservation of coherence between the person who chose law school and the person being shaped by it.

Fatigue Often Precedes Loss of Purpose

Purpose does not persist under sustained stress without maintenance. That is the reason why you must not be fazed when:

- early confusion gives way to self-doubt

- effort is expended long before results are visible

- feedback arrives late

- comparison becomes unavoidable

These conditions must not lead to you becoming disconnected from your "why." For non-traditional students, momentum cannot depend on enthusiasm. It depends on continuity that is maintained by:

- intentionally revisiting your "why"

- integrating it into ongoing decision-making

- using it as a reference point when evaluating setbacks

Actively remembering your "why" does not eliminate doubt. It contextualizes it, preventing temporary strain from becoming a permanent decision. As the saying goes, the hardship is temporary, but the law degree is permanent.

Each student ultimately decides how much truth that statement holds for them.

2.   HOW TO ACTIVELY REMEMBER YOUR WHY

Remembering your "why" is a practice, not a feeling. Constraint-driven students build reminders into their routines. This may include:

- writing your "why" somewhere visible

- revisiting the event, value, or responsibility that led you to law school

- measuring progress by alignment, not perfection

- reframing setbacks as part of preparation, not proof of inadequacy

Your "why" should be within reach for times of pressure peaks. Write it where you cannot avoid it: on your laptop, your desk, your mirror, your fridge, or your phone cover. When pressure rises, external cues, like this vision reminder, matter.

Make your vision plain.

Choose in advance to remember it during the most demanding weeks of law school, when exhaustion clouds perspective and persistence feels costly. Revisit it regularly. It will carry you through.

The Strategic Function of Remembering Your Why

Within the Constraint-Driven Method™, remembering your why operates as a stabilizing mechanism. It allows you to:

- absorb poor performance without overreacting

- rest without interpreting fatigue as defeat

- persist without needing constant reassurance

When your "why" is actively remembered, you stop recalibrating your commitment every time circumstances change. That stability becomes a competitive advantage.

This principle strengthens the Constraint-Driven Method™ by maintaining consistent action when stress threatens to fracture purpose.

8

SLEEP BEFORE YOU QUIT

Once your mind stops absorbing information, continuing to read, outline, or highlight does not make you more prepared, it makes you more exhausted. At that point, studying becomes performative rather than productive.

There is no academic benefit to studying past the point of retention. When your eyes are moving but your mind is not, the work is done for the day.

---

1.   GUILT KEEPS PEOPLE AWAKE

Most students do not stay up late because it is effective for them. They stay up because of guilt. They imagine their peers studying. They assume rest is weakness. They equate hours awake with commitment. So, they fight sleep even when they are not retaining the material.

However, guilt is not a stable study strategy.

Clocking hours that do not maximize retention is not discipline. It is waste. Remember that for a non-traditional student, studying is all about maximizing time and performance.

You have to incorporate sleep in your performance design.

A professor once said and I fully second it: *"When you feel like you can't do it anymore, it is time to close everything and go to bed."*

The Newborn Lesson

Anyone who has had a newborn has heard this advice from experienced parents or medical professionals:

"Sleep when the baby sleeps."

And almost every new parent, especially mothers, fight it. They think:
"This is the only time I can do laundry."
"This is when I can shower."
"This is when I can tidy up, do the dishes, catch up on a show, or finally breathe."

It feels rational. It feels productive. It is also misguided.

What happens instead is predictable: the baby wakes sooner than expected, the mother is still exhausted, more restless, less able to function. Often, the tasks she had hoped to complete are never completed. By resisting rest, she ends up doing less and being more tired.

Law school fatigue works the same way. So, be wise.

Fatigue Lies

When you are tired, your thoughts are unreliable. Fatigue tells you:
"I can't do this."
"I'm behind."
"Everyone else is doing better."
"This is not for me."
"I should quit."

These thoughts are not trustworthy. Anytime you have the thought "I can't do this anymore" *while exhausted*, do not act on it yet. Go to sleep.

2.   SLEEP RESTORES PERSPECTIVE

After rest, problems often look different; not because circumstances changed, but because *you did.*

Sleep restores:

- Memory consolidation

- Emotional regulation

- Judgment

Rest, so you can recover clarity when needed.

Endurance Requires Recovery

Law school is not survived through constant output. It is sustained through cycles of effort and recovery.

Students who respect their sleep time protect:

- Retention

- Confidence

- Decision-making

A Simple Rule

Before you spiral. Before you quit. Before you decide you are incapable. *Sleep first.* If the problem persists after rest, you can address it clearly. Most of the time, it will not.

3.   USE COUNSELING SERVICES

Fatigue impairs judgment before it produces visible collapse. Counseling services are designed to interrupt this cycle. The right support restores good judgment.

Most law schools provide confidential counseling as part of their institutional infrastructure. These services exist to stabilize cognitive and emotional functioning under sustained stress, not merely to respond after a crisis has occurred.

In addition to campus-based resources, bar associations and pro bono organizations often offer confidential counseling or support services tailored to law students. These programs recognize that legal training imposes unique pressures and that early intervention prevents downstream consequences.

Do your research and start using counseling services as an informed response to predictable strain. Constraint-driven students treat mental health support as part of their system. Getting help early helps with steadiness and consistent performance. Non-traditional students often carry extra pressure, which reduces their margin and speeds up burnout. Using counseling early helps protect your energy and supports clear decision-making when it matters most.

This principle strengthens the Constraint-Driven Method™ by treating rest as a strategic intervention—preserving retention, stabilizing emotions, and preventing fatigue-driven decisions.

OPERATIONAL SUMMARY: PART II

This part requires you to treat endurance as an operational requirement rather than a personal trait. You are expected to identify a functional purpose that sustains effort under pressure, protect sleep as a decision-making asset, and recognize when internal strain—not lack of ability— is driving doubt or disengagement.

Before proceeding, you should be able to distinguish between fatigue and failure, and you should have systems in place that preserve judgment when pressure increases.

PART III — PERFORMANCE EXECUTION

*"I did then what I knew how to do. Now that I know
better, I do better."* — **Maya Angelou**

9

STAY AHEAD, NOT CAUGHT UP

Non-traditional law students often define success in terms of survival. Keeping up. Staying afloat. Getting through. They often say: "with all that I have going, I am doing well just catching up." That mindset is understandable. When time is scarce and responsibilities are constant, survival can feel like the most realistic goal. But survival is a floor—it may keep you enrolled, but it does not produce the level of performance law school rewards.

---

1.   STAY AHEAD TO CREATE BUFFER

"Catching up" is a failing strategy. For non-traditional students, falling behind escalates quickly: time pressure intensifies, stress distorts judgment, mistakes multiply, and learning shifts from deliberate to reactive. Catching up typically requires relearning material under poor conditions, namely low energy, limited time, and heightened anxiety. That approach is inefficient and unnecessary.

Staying ahead is about *maintaining* buffer. Law school rewards anticipation. The students who perform best are not those who continuously react to setbacks, but those who problem-solve prior to problems arising in the first place. The objective is not to chase the curve. You must stay ahead of predictable friction points.

Anticipation Creates Margin

Staying ahead requires anticipating where problems typically arise and addressing them before they surface. Law school is predictable in this respect, as discussed below.

Exams follow patterns. Most law school exams present a long fact pattern containing multiple legal issues. The task is not simply to recall rules, but to identify the legal problems, explain the governing rule, and apply it to the facts.

Practical Example
A Civil Procedure exam might describe a car accident involving parties from different states, a lawsuit filed in a third state, and a contract connected to the dispute. The exam is not really about the story. It is about whether the student recognizes the embedded issues (personal jurisdiction, subject-matter jurisdiction, and venue) and organizes the answer around those issues.

Doctrinal confusion clusters around the same topics. Certain concepts repeatedly cause difficulty because they require analytical reasoning.

Practical Examples
In Torts, many students struggle with proximate cause and determining how far liability should extend when several events contribute to an injury.

In Criminal Law, students often struggle to distinguish between different intent standards when determining whether the defendant had the required mental state.

In Criminal Procedure, confusion frequently arises around the Fourth Amendment, especially determining when a police interaction becomes a search or a seizure and when a warrant or an exception to the warrant requirement applies.

In Civil Procedure, students often struggle with personal jurisdiction, especially the distinction between general jurisdiction and specific jurisdiction.

In Evidence, students often struggle with hearsay and the many exceptions to the hearsay rule. Exams frequently present statements made outside the courtroom and require students to determine whether the statement is hearsay, whether it is offered for the truth of the matter asserted, and whether an exception applies.

In Property, students often struggle with future interests and estates, including distinguishing among fee simple, life estates, remainders, and executory interests.

Performance dips occur at similar points each semester. Many students struggle during predictable moments in the academic cycle.

Practical Example
Early semester adjustment. New students initially struggle with reading appellate cases and extracting legal rules from judicial opinions.

Mid-semester overload. Around weeks five to eight, reading assignments accumulate across multiple courses, and students begin encountering more complex doctrinal frameworks.

Pre-exam realization. Many students discover that they understand individual cases but not the structure of the doctrine as a whole near the end of the semester.

By working strategically, you can:

- identify weaknesses before they appear on exams

- refine your approach while adjustment is still possible

- avoid relearning material under pressure

- reduce last-minute panic

Staying Ahead Does Not Require Doing More Than Everyone Else

Being ahead means doing the *right* work at the *right* time:

- clarifying expectations before exams are written

- identifying high-impact issues early

- correcting misunderstandings while they are still small

- allocating effort where it produces the greatest return

This approach conserves energy, protects focus, and supports steady progress without relying on unsustainable bursts of effort.

The shift from "getting through" to "staying ahead" is subtle but decisive. It reframes law school from a test of endurance into a system that can be navigated intelligently.

You are not here to barely survive. You are here to extract value from a demanding institution in the midst of real-life constraints. Staying ahead is how you do that.

Factor in Unpredictability

Non-traditional students are more likely to face sudden demands on their time: work emergencies, caregiving responsibilities, or health issues. For that reason, completing assignments ahead of schedule is not optional; it is protective. Being even a few days ahead creates a buffer when circumstances shift without warning.

Use Transitional Time Intentionally

Constraint-driven students recognize the value of transitional time and use it deliberately.

Workout sessions, commutes, school drop-offs, brief waiting periods, or other routine transitions can become opportunities for learning reinforcement. Audio materials, short lectures, or focused review tools can convert these otherwise idle moments into productive study time.

Teaching concepts aloud is particularly effective. Explaining a rule or doctrine whether to a child at bedtime or simply to yourself quickly reveals whether the concept is understood well enough to apply.

Staying ahead depends on building margin before it becomes necessary.

Because eventually, it will be.

2. START WITH A REALITY AUDIT

Effective execution begins with accurate inputs. You can only allocate effort properly if you are honest about your circumstances. When your strategy reflects reality, effort goes where it earns points, disruptions are easier to manage, and performance becomes more consistent.

Budget Time: Build a Truthful Calendar

Most students create aspirational schedules. Constraint-driven students must design systems that are sustainable. This requires a time audit. Until you know how your time is actually spent, you cannot manage or adjust it strategically. Many students underestimate time loss caused by unstructured screen time, task-switching, and low-energy work periods.

For at least one full week, track:

- when activities begin and end

- where time is spent and the outcome

- energy level at the start and end of each block

This data will produce a truthful calendar: one that reflects urgency, interruption, and recovery.
A schedule built on optimism collapses under pressure.

A schedule built on honesty absorbs shock.

Be Aware of the Institutional Baseline

Under the American Bar Association (ABA) guidance, law students are expected to complete approximately 42.5 hours of academic work per credit per semester, including class time, preparation, and assessment-related work. That is the equivalent of approximately 6-hours of study time every day for a full-time student. And this expectation exists regardless of a student's external responsibilities. Law schools typically suggest studying 2–3 hours for every class hour.

A truthful calendar is therefore not a preference; it is a compliance check. You have to take the institutional workload expectations into consideration alongside the actual hours available in your week. Scheduling remains aspirational rather than operational until you do.

Energy Cycles: Match Work to Capacity

Energy is not evenly distributed across the day, and it is not infinitely renewable. Most students assume they can perform cognitively demanding work whenever time appears available. Not true.

You must identify:

- periods of sustained focus

- periods of moderate productivity

- periods of cognitive fatigue

High-concentration work which includes exam practice, rule memorization, and analytical outlining must be reserved for narrow windows of peak capacity. Reading, briefing, reviewing, and administrative tasks belong elsewhere.

Ignoring energy cycles produces inefficiency and false conclusions about ability. Designing with these cycles in mind increases accuracy and preserves judgment.

Family and Work Obligations: Fix Them in Your Operating Environment

Constraint-driven planning treats family and employment responsibilities as structural facts, not obstacles to overcome. For example, pick-up times, work shifts, caregiving duties, and household obligations must be placed on the calendar. If you do not acknowledge family or work in your study plan, you may end up constantly behind.

Non-Negotiables: Do Not Violate Them

Non-negotiables are commitments that cannot be moved, shortened, or sacrificed without real consequence. These may include health needs or social obligations.

Many students treat non-negotiables as flexible until a crisis forces them not to. Constraint-driven students identify them early and protect them intentionally.

Foreseeable Risk Points: Do not Negotiate Them

Every semester contains predictable pressure points:

- midterms

- clustered deadlines

- illness seasons

- work surges

- personal transitions

- family disruptions

Effective systems anticipate these points and build a buffer in advance. This may mean front-loading work, reducing commitments temporarily, or planning recovery time ahead of time.

Performance rarely collapses due to inability. It collapses when systems are designed for conditions that are contrary to reality. Constraint analysis is the step that turns intention into strategy.

3.   TAKE ADVANTAGE OF ORIENTATION WEEK

As a new law student, one of your first priorities is to understand how law school works quickly so you can start using effective strategies right away.

Attend as Many Orientation Sessions as Your Schedule Reasonably Allows

Orientation settings matter because professors and administrators are often at their most candid. They share expectations, common pitfalls, and practical guidance that rarely appear in syllabi. Orientation sessions are also an opportunity to learn about affinity groups, institutional resources, and potential mentors if you do not already have one. Use this time to understand the structure of your institution.

Introduce yourself to the Dean of Student Affairs early. For non-traditional students, this office is often the primary point of support when life intervenes unexpectedly. Familiarity established before a crisis arises makes communication easier and more effective later. If the opportunity presents itself, meet senior administrators as well. There is no downside to being known professionally within the institution you are navigating.

When your school hosts events for new students, block time to attend. These are not social add-ons; they are part of your institutional onboarding. They help you understand law school culture, norms, and expectations. This is information that reduces friction later.

4.   BLOCK DISTRACTIONS BEFORE THEY OVERCOME YOU

Staying ahead in law school is also about protecting attention.

Distraction is rarely accidental. It is engineered, normalized, and socially reinforced. Notifications, social media, constant availability, and background noise create a state of perpetual reactivity. Students who stay ahead do not rely solely on willpower. They design their environments to reduce distractions before pressure peaks.

When attention is fragmented, it is tempting to study only when deadlines force you to. You respond instead of anticipating. You spend more time switching tasks than completing them. For non-traditional students, whose time and energy are already constrained, this can be expensive.

Rebuilding Attention for Endurance

Even when distractions are reduced, many students struggle to *sustain* focus. This is not a failure of discipline or intelligence. It is the result of conditioning.

Nowadays, most students arrive at law school after years of exposure to short-form content—one-to-two-minute videos, rapid scrolling, constant novelty. These platforms train attention to expect immediate stimulation and frequent reward. Law school demands the opposite: prolonged concentration, delayed payoff, and tolerance for cognitive discomfort.

The mismatch is jarring.

Legal study involves working through dense material, following complex arguments, and staying with uncertainty for long periods. Students who are not used to this often mistake fatigue for lack of ability and disengage too early.

Attention endurance is not innate. It is developed. Building attention endurance requires deliberate practice: gradually extending uninterrupted study sessions, limiting task-switching, and remaining with the work even when discomfort appears. This adjustment must occur early. Waiting until reading loads increase and examinations approach forces adaptation under urgency. At that time, cognitive strain is already elevated.

For non-traditional students, whose study windows are inherently constrained, the ability to concentrate deeply for sustained periods creates a buffer. A few hours that produce high-quality work are likely to preserve margin before deadlines compress options.

Staying ahead also requires uninterrupted time to think, synthesize, and prepare before urgency sets in. Distraction collapses that margin and shifts work from planned execution to reactive completion.

Respect For Limited Capacity

Non-traditional students cannot afford attention leakage. Students with unlimited time may recover from distraction. Non-traditional students cannot easily do the same.

When study time is compressed by work, family, or other responsibilities, every interruption carries a cost. Five minutes lost is rarely just five minutes; it breaks momentum, delays comprehension, and increases fatigue.

Blocking distractions is about respect for limited capacity.

Establish Focus Boundaries

You must self-impose restrictions to achieve your goals. Distraction controls should be established before the semester begins—or before academic pressure intensifies.

Decide in advance when your phone will be inaccessible, which applications or websites will be restricted, where focused study will take place, and who should or should not have access to you during study windows. Consider limiting social media and entertainment platforms unless they serve a *clear* educational purpose, such as participating in learning communities.

Make these decisions while you are calm, not when you are overwhelmed. Once pressure escalates, boundaries become harder to impose. Systems established early continue to function even when discipline weakens.

You must therefore protect uninterrupted time deliberately. Phones are placed out of reach, notifications are disabled, and digital platforms that invite distraction are restricted during study blocks. The goal is simple: prevent unnecessary interruptions from eroding the buffer required for consistent performance.

Students who protect their attention span finish tasks faster, retain more, and experience less panic. They appear composed not because they are less busy, but because they are less fragmented.

Blocking distractions is about doing what matters without interference.

Staying Ahead Protects Confidence

One of the hidden costs of constantly catching up is erosion of confidence. When you are always reacting, it is easy to internalize struggle as inadequacy. Staying ahead interrupts that narrative.

For non-traditional students, this matters because confidence stabilizes performance when external pressures intensify.

5.   LEARN HOW TO READ

It sounds strange, but you must learn how to read again. Reading in law school is a different skill. You have to improve your ability to read to go through cases quickly and intelligently. The best training method is to practice with real judicial opinions.

Several public databases allow you to download them for free:

- CourtListener

- Google Scholar (Case Law section)

- Cornell Law School's Legal Information Institute (LII)

- Oyez

- Justia

Using these sources, you can download several opinions and practice extracting the key elements of a case.

The Six-Minute Rule

The *six-minute rule* trains you not to read every sentence carefully, but to identify the structure of the decision quickly.

Read the last paragraph first (about 30 seconds). The final section usually states the court's holding. It signals whether the decision is affirmed, reversed, or remanded. Look for language like:

"We hold that…"
"The court concludes…"
"The judgment is affirmed/reversed…"

Once you know the holding, the rest of the opinion becomes easier to interpret because you now know what the court decided.

Identify the issue (about 30 seconds). Scan the opening section or early paragraphs for the legal question. Often phrased as:

"The question before the court is…"
"This case requires us to decide whether…"

This gives you the legal problem the court is solving.

Locate the rule (about one minute). Next, locate the section where the court explains the governing law. This usually appears in phrases such as:

"Courts consider several factors…"
"To establish x…"
"Under the doctrine of…"
"The test for determining…"
"The standard for…"

This is the legal standard the court will apply.

Scan the key facts (about two minutes). Read the facts, but only with one question in mind: which facts matter for the rule? Ignore background details that do not relate to the issue. In many opinions, only a few facts actually determine the outcome.

Read the reasoning (about two minutes). The reasoning explains:

How the court applies the rule to the facts;
Why the court reaches a particular conclusion.

This is the analysis section, which is the *most important* part of the case.

After six minutes, you should be able to write five short lines describing the case: Facts. Issue. Rule. Reasoning. Holding. It takes a lot of practice to master this skill. But practicing this method regularly will help you move from slow reading to strategic reading. The goal is not speed alone, but the ability to identify the structure that produces the legal outcome.

Use this simple daily drill:

- Download 1–5 opinions

- Start with appellate opinions between 5–10 pages

- Avoid long Supreme Court opinions (they are often 40–80 pages)

- Spend no more than 10 minutes per case

- Extract only: basic facts, issue(s), rule(s), holding, reasoning

Once classes start, you will have an overwhelmingly large number of cases assigned. But if you practice reading beforehand, you will have a strategic advantage.

Always Read with Purpose

For each course, use your syllabus and casebook's table of contents to understand the doctrinal unit you are entering. Law school assigns a volume of reading that is deliberately unrealistic if approached linearly. This is not by accident. It is a filtering mechanism. The system is testing your ability to extract what matters.

Read to identify rules, reasoning patterns, and doctrinal movement. As you read, ask and answer these questions mechanically:

- What question is the court answering?

- Why does this question matter doctrinally?

- What legal test, rule, or principle emerges?

- How is it applied?

- Why did the court reach this result?

- What facts were outcome-determinative?

- How could this rule be tested on a final exam?

- What factual variation would flip the result?

Once you can articulate those elements, you have effectively extracted the value of the reading.

Strategic Reading Prepares the Most for Cold Calling

Cold calling is a common feature of law school classrooms. Professors randomly ask students to explain the facts of a case, identify the legal issue, describe the rule, or analyze how the court reached its decision. Or even when you ask a question, the response may be: "You tell me," placing you on the spot.

For students who read cases without structure, cold calling can feel unpredictable and intimidating. However, most cold calls focus on the same predictable points.

Strategic reading prepares you for these questions automatically. When you read a case with the goal of identifying the facts, issue, rule, reasoning, and holding, you are already preparing the answers most professors are likely to ask.

The purpose of cold calling is not to embarrass students. It is to train them to think on their feet, think through legal problems aloud, and to understand how legal reasoning unfolds step by step.

When you read strategically, cold calling becomes less about surprise and more about confirming that you understood the structure of the case.

The Three-Sentence Rule

A simple way to answer cold calls and check whether you truly understood a case is to follow the *three-sentence rule*.

If you understand a judicial opinion, you should be able to explain it in three clear sentences:

Sentence 1: What happened and what the court had to decide.
Sentence 2: The rule the court applied or the legal principle that controlled the decision.
Sentence 3: What the court decided and why.

If you cannot summarize a case this way, you probably read the opinion but did not yet understand its structure.

The purpose of reading cases in law school is not to memorize every detail of the narrative (although some of their fact pattern may inform those of the final exam's). It is to understand how courts move from facts, to rule, to decision. The three-sentence rule forces you to critically think.

Practical Example

Sentence 1: A customer slipped on a wet floor in a grocery store, and the court had to decide whether the store could be liable for negligence.

Sentence 2: A business is liable for negligence when it fails to exercise reasonable care to keep its premises safe for customers.

Sentence 3: The court held the store liable because employees knew about the spill and failed to clean it or warn customers.

If you can reduce a case to these three sentences, you have extracted every part that matters.

6.   INCORPORATE SUPPLEMENTS

The Constraint-Driven Method™ governs *strategy and system design*. Academic supplements address substance and mechanics. When used appropriately, they can support doctrinal learning, outlining, and exam preparation.

Supplements are *not* substitutes for judgment, performance design, or alignment with faculty expectations. Their value is conditional. They are most effective once a student understands how assessment operates in a particular course and what signals individual professors reward. Used prematurely or indiscriminately, they often increase noise rather than clarity.

The resources below are commonly used to explain law school mechanics. They do not dictate strategy, neither do they override professor-specific priorities.

BOOKS THAT CLARIFY LAW SCHOOL ASSESSMENT MECHANICS

These books are best used to understand how law school evaluates performance, not to build a full study system. Read selectively, at the right time, and resist the urge to adopt every tactic.

- *Getting to Maybe* by Richard Michael Fischl & Jeremy Paul

- *Succeeding in Law School* by Herbert N. Ramy

- *1L of a Ride* by Andrew J. McClurg

- *Law School Confidential* by Robert H. Miller

- *The Glannon Guide to Law School Exams* by Joseph T. McClurg

- *Thinking Like a Lawyer* by Frederick Schauer

- *Learning to Think Like a Lawyer* by Elizabeth Mertz

There are other alternatives out there. Do your research. Remember to choose according to your circumstances.

HORNBOOKS

Hornbooks are most effective to clarify doctrine that has already been introduced in class. They should not replace case reading, class preparation, or professor-specific guidance. The following list reflects commonly used options.

Doctrine Clarification & Application—These are most useful after class to confirm understanding.

- *Examples & Explanations* Widely used across doctrinal courses (Contracts, Torts, Civil Procedure, Property, Criminal Law, etc.). Best for testing comprehension through hypotheticals.

- *Gilbert Law Summaries* Useful for high-level structure and rule organization, particularly for review.

- *CrunchTime* Includes outlines, flowcharts, and practice questions. Best used for exam orientation.

Orientation & Conceptual Framing—These are helpful when a subject feels unfamiliar or abstract.

- *Short & Happy Guide Series* Plain-language introductions to doctrinal subjects. Useful early in a course to establish context and vocabulary.

- *Acing* Focuses on how specific subjects are tested rather than full doctrinal coverage.

Legal Reasoning & Skills—These supplements focus less on doctrine and more on *how* lawyers think and write.

- *Legal Reasoning and Legal Writing* Commonly used in legal writing programs. Helpful for understanding analytical structure and clarity.

- *Plain English for Lawyers* Useful for improving clarity and precision in legal writing. Not exam-focused, but valuable for long-term skill development.

- *Making Your Case* Focuses on persuasion and argument structure. More relevant after foundational skills are in place.

Practice Questions & Exam Technique—These are best used after students understand what professors are testing.

- *Glannon Guide* Helpful for translating doctrine into exam-ready reasoning.

- *Friedland's Techniques* Focuses on exam strategy and performance mechanics. Useful after first-semester feedback.

DIGITAL SUPPLEMENT PLATFORMS

Some students prefer digital formats. These should be used cautiously to avoid volume overload.

- *West Academic Online*

- *LexisNexis Digital Study Aids*

- *CALI Lessons*

Digital tools can support targeted review but often encourage over-consumption if not tightly bounded.

That said, not all supplements align with how a particular professor teaches or grades.

The best practice is simple: Ask your professors which resources they suggest their students use because using a supplement they recommend will be far more valuable than using a popular one they ignore.

Video-based Resources

In addition to traditional supplements, video-based resources can be effective time-savers when used selectively.

Platforms such as Quimbee, educational YouTube channels, and Themis (or other Bar Prep programs) 1L and 2L doctrinal videos can help:

- Preview a topic before class

- Clarify structure after class

- Explain black-letter law

- Illustrate cases in more accessible ways

These resources are best understood as efficiency tools that help with reinforcing concepts, previewing unfamiliar material, or resolving confusion quickly. They do *not* replace primary sources, class instruction, or professor-specific expectations. Used appropriately and in alignment with course objectives, video tools can reduce friction without distorting focus.

Audio and Reading-Assist Tools

Some students look to audio or reading-assist applications to manage dense assignments more efficiently:

- Text-to-speech platforms such as *Speechify* or *NaturalReader* can be effective for second-pass exposure to cases, statutes, or supplemental materials, particularly when time or energy is limited.

- Visual reading aids like *BeeLine Reader* may help sustain focus during dense readings.

Generative Artificial Intelligence

When used appropriately, the collaborative use of artificial intelligence to *support* learning can function as a study partner to clarify doctrine or test understanding

The problem is not assistance. The problem is *substitution*. Legal education is designed to measure a student's independent reasoning, judgment, and ability to perform under constraint. Any tool, human or technological, that replaces that reasoning undermines the very credential the system is built to confer.

Strategic students use tools to enhance comprehension, *not* to *outsource* thinking. Used correctly, AI can accelerate learning. Used carelessly, it can obscure weaknesses until the moment performance is required; by then, it will be too late. You must also know how law schools are responding:

- Academic integrity policies and honor codes have been updated. Many honor codes now explicitly classify undisclosed AI use as unauthorized assistance. You must check the rules at your institution.
- Assessment design has changed. Professors are increasingly using closed-network or locked-browser exams.
- Faculty rely on pattern recognition. Professors compare exam answers to prior work, in-class writing, and oral performance. Writing that is overly generic, unnaturally polished, or detached from the actual prompt is often more suspicious than work that is imperfect but responsive.

- Some schools now pair written submissions with oral explanations, use in-class timed writing as verification, and compare exam writing to a student's prior work for consistency.
- However, some schools have also embraced the use of AI for upper-level courses that are less doctrinal but more skills based.

A Caution on Overuse

Supplements are reference tools, not authorities. They help you see the *shape* of the law after you have engaged with class material. They do not replace the reading assignments. If a supplement conflicts with your professor's framing, the supplement is wrong *for your purposes*.

There is no way around doing the work

Over-supplementation creates the illusion of preparation. If you could not reproduce the work unaided, or explain a rule in your own words, or apply it to a new fact pattern, the supplement has been misused, and you are doing yourself a disfavor.

How to Choose

You do not need every supplement under the sun. Most students benefit from just *one* primary supplement per course, selected based on:

- how the professor tests and what the professor recommends

- where confusion arises

- how the student processes information under constraint

More materials do not produce better results. Better alignment does. Hornbooks and supplements explain content and mechanics. They do not design *performance systems*.

7.   REFINE YOUR STRENGTHS

One persistent myth in legal education is that excellence requires uniformity. Students often assume they must perform equally well across every skill.

That is not true.

You may discover that written advocacy comes more naturally than oral advocacy, or that multiple-choice questions produce stronger results than essay responses. While you must prepare adequately for all required exam formats, the greatest return often comes from refining the mode of performance that consistently produces results.

Refining a strength does three things at once:

- It increases consistency of high performance

- It reduces cognitive and emotional load

- It creates margin when other areas fluctuate

The goal is to leverage strengths so effectively that weaknesses do not control outcomes. Strategic success begins with understanding the strengths and limitations you bring into law school and refining them deliberately.

8.   USE THIS FORMULA TO REMAIN AHEAD

Excellence in law school is attainable for non-traditional students when effort is structured deliberately. Staying ahead requires following consistent steps that yield consistent results:

- *Create Earlier Deadlines for Yourself* to build a safety net against unpredictability.

- *Always Study with Purpose* to save yourself from dispersing effort across everything that appears important.

- *Avoid Over-Briefing* because excess detail increases workload without improving performance.

- *Use Supplements Selectively* to resolve confusion or reinforce organization, not to replace engagement with the course.

- *Use Class Time and Office Hours* to confirm or correct your understanding.

- *Take Notes That Reflect What the Professor Emphasizes* as it often appears on the final exam.

- *Draft Your Own Outlines* at the conclusion of each doctrinal unit while the material is still fresh. Reviewing others' outlines may help with structure, but synthesis *must* be *yours*.

- *Commit Core Rules and Frameworks to Memory Every Week* to prevent end-of-semester compression.

This principle strengthens the Constraint-Driven Method™ by preserving momentum and reducing avoidable pressure through anticipatory action under real-world operating conditions.

10

SEEK HELP BEFORE YOU NEED IT

Academic problems do not announce themselves loudly. They accumulate quietly. By the time a student realizes something is wrong, the window to correct their course may be almost closed. That is the reason you must proactively seek help to gauge whether you are on the right track or take adequate corrective measures.

---

1.   HELP IS MOST VALUABLE BEFORE FAILURE

One frequent mistake that non-traditional students make is waiting too long to seek clarification and failing to ask questions that actually matter. I am referring to questions that shape outcomes.

At one end of the spectrum, students delay asking for help. They assume they should "figure it out themselves," wait for grades to confirm their understanding, or hesitate out of misplaced professionalism or fear of appearing unprepared. By the time they act, feedback has already arrived in its most expensive form.

At the other end are students who worry too early about everything and seek constant reassurance. This behavior is often misread as insecurity. In reality, it frequently reflects situational awareness: an understanding of one's circumstances, learning style, and limited tolerance for inefficiency. The problem is not seeking reassurance but seeking it indiscriminately.

The goal is neither silence nor constant reassurance. The goal is timely, targeted clarification, as in questions that reduce uncertainty and align effort with evaluation.

First-year grades matter disproportionately, and the cost of delayed or unfocused inquiry accumulates quickly. Do not wait for grades to tell you something is wrong. Seek clarity early, seek it deliberately.

Law School Operates on Delayed Feedback

You often do not know whether your approach is working until an exam has already been graded. At that point, weeks or an entire semester may have been lost. Seeking help early functions as *preventive action*.

Early questions:

- can correct misunderstandings before they harden into habits
- clarify expectations while adjustments are still possible
- reduce the risk of misallocating time and effort

Late questions, by contrast, are often remedial. They aim to repair damage rather than prevent it.

Non-traditional students cannot afford that inefficiency.

Early Help Builds Strategic Visibility

Many non-traditional students isolate themselves to their disadvantage.

Law schools are institutions operated by people, and discretion is exercised every day by faculty, administrators, and support staff.

Students who engage early and professionally are easier to assist because their effort, consistency, and context are already understood. Early visibility establishes credibility before pressure escalates or crises arise.

Introduce yourself early without oversharing. Explain your circumstances without apology. Ask questions with intent. Treat support as infrastructure, not as a last resort.

The Professional Misconception

Many non-traditional students arrive at law school with substantial professional credentials. In prior environments, independence was often rewarded. Asking questions early may have been unnecessary or even discouraged.

What I refer to as *the professional misconception* often appears in two forms: the "Paralegal Syndrome" and the "PhD Complex."

Paralegals work closely with attorneys and are already fluent in legal language and procedure. Similarly, doctorate holders are trained researchers who have produced original scholarship and lengthy theses. Both groups bring genuine strengths into law school. Yet those strengths are sometimes misapplied in the early stages of legal education.

Prior familiarity with the legal field, or prior success in academia, can create an *illusory advantage*. It is the early impression that one already understands how legal reasoning and evaluation operate. Some students assume they can write legal arguments according to their own analytical preferences without adhering to established methods of legal analysis and writing. Others assume that professional competence will translate directly into academic success.

It does not.

Law school is not a workplace where performance is measured by output according to personal criteria. It is an evaluative system governed by:

- implicit expectations

- defined analytical methods

- professor-specific preferences

- grading curves

- institutional norms

You are not expected to intuit these rules. You are expected to learn them.

Any advantage conferred by prior exposure to the law is often temporary. Familiarity may soften the initial transition, but it does not determine long-term outcomes. As the semesters progress, evaluation shifts away from comfort with legal language and toward disciplined analysis, structured application, and exam execution. Students who rely on background without adaptation eventually plateau. Students who deliberately build skill catch up and often outperform their peers.

Professional experience functions as an asset only when paired with humility and adaptability. Do not assume your background exempts you from learning the system you have entered. Prior exposure may influence the starting position, but in law school it does not determine the finish line. What determines the finish line is not background, but whether a student learns to operate within the structure of the system itself.

What Counts as "Seeking Help"

Strategic help-seeking is targeted and intentional. It includes:

- clarifying how a professor approaches exams

- confirming whether your understanding of doctrine is accurate

- asking whether your study method aligns with course expectations

- checking assumptions before investing significant time

These questions are most effective when asked *before* stakes escalate.

The Cost of Waiting

Students who wait to ask questions often do so for understandable reasons:

- they do not want to draw attention

- they believe others understand more than they do

- they assume confusion will resolve itself

Unfortunately, confusion rarely resolves by itself and without intervention. By the time students seek help, deadlines have passed, patterns are entrenched, and options are limited. The result is not always failure—but it is often underperformance that could have been avoided.

2.   MASTER WHAT MATTERS

High performance in law school is not produced by equal attention to all material. It is produced by disciplined focus on what the institution actually evaluates.

In doctrinal courses, the primary measurable outcome is exam performance. Grades, class rank, and academic standing flow directly from exams and shape access to opportunities, credibility, and early career positioning.

In skills-based courses, performance is measured through written and oral advocacy—legal analysis, research, and communication demonstrated in memos, briefs, motions, and structured oral exercises.

MASTER WHAT TO STUDY

Law school exams reward a narrow set of competencies and repeatedly test a narrow band of material. They do not reward volume of work. Reading, outlining, and briefing have value *only* to the extent they strengthen these exam-facing skills.

Accordingly, you must identify and master high-yield material, including:

- core doctrinal rules

- recurring issue patterns

- analytical frameworks emphasized by the professor

- application-heavy concepts that demonstrate reasoning

High-yield material is not hidden. It surfaces through:

- syllabus emphasis

- hypotheticals discussed in class

- prior exams

- model answers

Students who learn to read these signals stop guessing. Their preparation becomes targeted.

Calibrate to the Evaluator

A professor does not grade based on how hard you worked, how much you read, or how strongly you felt about the material. They grade based on their own criteria, communicated through syllabi, lectures, feedback, and prior exams. Since grading is professor-specific, mastery must therefore be calibrated to how *each* professor evaluates performance.

You must determine:

- how questions are structured

- what level of detail is rewarded

- whether precision, synthesis, or policy carries more weight

- how organization is scored relative to substance

Ignoring evaluator preferences is one of the most common reasons capable students underperform. Office hours and early feedback are data sources, not reassurance sessions.

Depth Over Breadth

Mastery is demonstrated through analysis, not recognition. Knowledge of a rule is insufficient unless you can:

- articulate it clearly

- apply it accurately to facts

- distinguish it when appropriate

- deploy it efficiently under time pressure

Deprioritize Strategically

Every course contains material that is low yield. Constraint-driven students must decide deliberately what *not* to prioritize. This is not negligence. It is strategy. De-prioritization frees time and energy for:

- exam practice

- refining analysis

- targeted review

- recovery

When resources are limited, allocation matters more than effort.

MASTER HOW TO EXECUTE

Understanding what matters is not enough. You must practice under the conditions in which performance is evaluated.

Every exam is governed by:

- time limits

- question format

- grading rubrics

A study method that works in unlimited time may fail entirely under timed conditions. Preparation must mirror evaluation.

Effective practice includes:

- exam-style questions

- timed execution

- deliberate answer structure

- comparison with model answers

Diagnose, Then Correct

Reviewing practice work exposes common weaknesses:

- missed issues

- weak rule articulation

- disorganized analysis

- poor time allocation

Without practice and review, such errors often remain invisible until the exam itself. Honest self-assessment—free from defensiveness—is essential. Accuracy, speed, and structural clarity are the variables that ultimately determine exam performance.

The Curve Defines the Objective

Most law school courses are graded on a curve. Performance is *ranked*, not assessed in isolation.

As a result:

- multiple students may write competent exams, but only a few receive top grades

- improvement does not always translate into immediate grade movement

- small differences in structure, prioritization, and clarity often determine rank

The objective is not to know everything. It is to outperform peers on the specific skills being tested.

IRAC Method as Grading Infrastructure

Most exams are graded anonymously. Only what appears on the page matters. Because graders must score large volumes efficiently, analysis must be legible and structured. Issue, Rule, Application, and Conclusion (IRAC) functions as grading infrastructure:

- Issue identification opens access to points

- Rule articulation establishes credibility

- Application earns the majority of points

- Conclusions provide closure, not weight

Correct reasoning that is poorly structured often goes unrewarded. Clear structure allows even partial understanding to earn credit.

Rule of Engagement: Precision Over Accumulation

Work that does not improve exam performance or advance defined career goals should be questioned or set aside. When effort is aligned with evaluation, performance stabilizes, stress decreases, and results become repeatable.

Your rule of engagement should be *OMP* all semester long consistently, not occasionally, as follows:

- Outlining

- Memorizing

- Practicing

Outlining is the process of organizing legal material into a structured, usable format that mirrors how exam answers are written. It is not a summary of cases or class notes. It distills the course into rules, issues, and analytical frameworks that can be quickly recalled and applied under time constraints.

Outlines should be built based on how exams are answered rather than on lectures or case chronology. Under constraint, they must be usable instantly. Develop a second, condensed version for exams (sometimes called an attack outline) that guide issue spotting and analysis. If your outline cannot direct your answer under time pressure, it is not functional.

A functional outline:

- organizes content by legal issues and governing rules

- highlights how those rules apply to facts

- eliminates low-value detail

- allows for quick navigation during preparation and execution

The purpose of outlining is not to record what was taught. It is to prepare how you will perform. As you outline, you should be memorizing at the same time. Do not wait until the outline is complete before committing it to memory.

Memorization converts your outline into usable performance. Rules should be learned in a format that leads directly into analysis: use an element-based approach (applies when a rule is broken into required components that must all be satisfied) or a framework-based approach (applies when the rule is not a checklist, but a set of factors or balancing considerations).

Each of these approaches forces application. Memorizing rules in isolation is insufficient; you must be able to use them immediately and clearly. Because exams are typically typed, memorization should be practiced through typing. This builds both recall and fluency, so that rules can be retrieved and expressed without hesitation.

If your memorization does not already contain the path to application, it will break down under time pressure. Memorization should extend your outline into execution—it should already reflect how the rule will be used in an answer.

Practicing builds fluency under pressure and exposes weaknesses early. Start practicing under exam conditions early to expose gaps that passive review cannot reveal.

Again, outline, memorize, PRACTICE!

MASTER THE ANATOMY OF A LAW SCHOOL EXAM

When you open a law school exam, you will see (1) a dense fact pattern—often two to three pages long—filled with details, events, and characters and (2) the call of the question.

Not every fact matters. Some facts are signals while others are noise. Your task is never to retell the story. You must identify the legal problems embedded in it and analyze them under time pressure *according* to the call of the question.

Pay Attention to the Call of the Question

There are different types of calls of the question. The most common are:

- Open-ended calls require you to identify and analyze all relevant issues, e.g., "Discuss all claims and defenses"; "Analyze the parties' rights and liabilities."

- Focused calls limit you to a specific issue or claim, e.g., "Did Dan commit assault?"; "Is the contract enforceable?"

- Dual-sided calls require analysis from both perspectives, e.g., "What arguments can each party make?"; "Analyze both sides."

- Mixed calls combine issue spotting with a required conclusion, e.g., "Discuss all claims. Which party is likely to prevail?"

Each format changes how you allocate time and structure your answer. Common errors with regard to the call of the question are:

- ignoring part of the question

- answering too broadly or too narrowly

- failing to address both sides when required

- writing without a clear conclusion when one is asked

Students often lose points because they answer the wrong question. Read the call carefully. Then answer exactly what is asked—no more, no less. There is no value in expanding beyond the call. You will just waste valuable time.

The call of the question guides you to:

- define the scope of your answer

- identify legally significant facts

- determine which issues matter most

- state the relevant rules clearly

- apply the rules that matter to the facts in a structured way

It does not reward memorization alone. It rewards disciplined analysis.

How to Start the Exam

Do not start writing immediately.

Read the fact pattern once for structure
Identify parties, relationships, and timeline.

Read again to identify issues
Ask: what legal problems are being tested?

Mark triggering facts
Facts are not random—they exist to trigger specific rules.

Outline on the spot before you write
Your outline is your roadmap. Spend a few minutes listing issues in order of importance.

The risk in skipping these steps is that your answer may be disorganized and incomplete. If you practice under exam conditions consistently, this will be easy as you will recognize some of the issues and their corresponding analyses.

Issue Spotting Under Pressure

Not every issue deserves equal time. Some are central. Others are distractions. Focus on what matters in the facts:

- Patterns similar to assigned readings

- Repeated or emphasized facts are often important

- Unusual or conflicting facts often signal an issue

- Clean, straightforward facts often test basic rules

- Extra detail may exist to distract or test judgment

Your job is to distinguish between what must be addressed and what can be left aside.

What and How to Write

Your answer should follow the IRAC structure. Always keep in mind that the analysis (the application of the rules to the facts) is where most points are earned. Do not recite rules without applying them, summarize facts without legal analysis, or write everything you know. Write only what moves the analysis forward.

- Begin with "The issue is whether…" and frame the precise legal question.

- Start your rule section with "Under…" and articulate the controlling legal standard clearly and concisely.

- Start your analysis with "Here…" and analyze the facts by explicitly linking them to the rule, using multiple "because" statements to show causation, reasoning, and legal significance.

- Conclude with "Therefore…" and directly answer the issue.

Your analysis must not merely describe facts—it must explain outcomes. Use "because" repeatedly to demonstrate why each fact matters, how it satisfies (or fails) the rule, and how it drives the conclusion.

Practical Example
The issue is whether the grocery store is liable for negligence after a customer slipped on a wet floor.

Under negligence law, a business is liable when it fails to exercise reasonable care to keep its premises safe for customers, including addressing or warning of known hazards.

Here, the store is liable because the floor was wet, creating a clear risk of slipping, because employees knew about the spill, and because they did nothing to fix it or warn customers. This shows a lack of reasonable care because a prudent store would have cleaned the spill or provided a warning.

Therefore, the grocery store is liable for negligence because it failed to exercise reasonable care after becoming aware of the hazard.

Time Management

Do not expect to finish the exam perfectly. You are expected to allocate time intelligently. Factor in nerves. It is common to freeze, even briefly, at the start. You may know the rules and the structure yet hesitate for a moment. If that happens, reset quickly and begin. Do not linger in that pause.

Once you start writing:

- Spend more time on high-value issues

- Do not get stuck over-analyzing one section

- Move when time requires it

Running out of time is quite common. Leaving major issues unaddressed is costly. What is not written cannot be graded.

If You Are Running Out of Time

Adjust immediately:

- switch to shorter, direct analysis

- state rules and apply them briefly

- touch remaining major issues, even if minimally

A partial answer across all major issues scores higher than a perfect answer on only one.

What Not to Do

- do not chase every possible issue

- do not write without a structure

- do not treat all issues equally

- do not confuse volume with quality

The exam rewards judgment as much as knowledge.

What to Expect Overall

The exam will feel overwhelming at first. That is by design.

But it is not random. It follows patterns:

- issues are embedded in facts

- rules are triggered by those facts

- performance depends on how you organize and apply them

Once you understand this, the exam becomes manageable. You are not being tested on how much you know, but on how well you can identify, prioritize, and analyze under time constraints. That is why consistent practice under timed conditions is essential.

Unstructured studying fails because knowledge alone is not enough. Performance depends on whether that knowledge can be deployed within the conditions of the exam.

Once you understand the anatomy of the exam, preparation changes. Studying is no longer about covering more material. It becomes about recognizing patterns, practicing structured analysis, and building speed and clarity under time constraints.

The exam is predictable. It is patterned, and those patterns can be learned, practiced, and executed.

MASTER ADVOCACY SKILLS

From the first weeks of law school, students are evaluated on written and oral analysis. Advocacy is not about being "good at writing" or "comfortable at speaking." It is about demonstrating legal judgment.

Legal writing courses and advocacy assignments are often misunderstood at the outset as opportunities for creativity, voice, or personal expression. However, these assignments are not graded on effort, elegance, eloquence, or originality in the abstract.

Across formats, evaluators are asking the same questions they ask on exams:

- Did you identify the correct issues?

- Did you select the governing rules accurately?

- Did you apply those rules coherently to the facts?

- Did you structure the analysis so it could be assessed efficiently?

- Did you exercise judgment about what mattered and what did not?

Structure Determines Credit

Like exams, legal advocacy is not graded holistically. Evaluators do not simply form a general impression of whether an argument "feels strong." Instead, they assess specific components: identifying issues, stating rules, applying those rules to facts, addressing counterarguments, and organizing analysis coherently.

Credit is allocated across these discrete elements. Structure makes that evaluation possible. When analysis is organized clearly, evaluators can locate each component and assign credit accordingly. When reasoning appears in unstructured prose, even correct ideas may go unrecognized because the evaluator cannot easily identify the analytical steps being assessed.

When structure is missing, even sound reasoning may go uncredited because it cannot be identified efficiently. However, when structure is present, even partial understanding can earn points because the analysis is legible.

Knowledge that cannot be evaluated does not score.

Whether the task is:

- a closed memorandum

- an open research assignment

- a motion

- a brief

- a demand letter

- or an oral argument

the institution rewards the same thing: clear legal analysis presented in a structure that aligns with how performance is evaluated.

Structure does more than improve readability. It determines whether the work receives credit.

Research Is Evaluated Through Use, Not Accumulation

Do not fall for the trap of treating research as an end in itself. Legal research is not graded by how much authority you find. It is graded by how effectively you select and deploy the authority that matters. Excess citations do not strengthen an argument if they are not integrated. Long case strings do not substitute for judgment.

Professors, judges, and supervising attorneys evaluate research through the same lens:

- relevance

- precision

- judgment

The question is not whether you worked hard. The question is whether you chose what mattered and used it correctly for your specific set of facts.

Writing Makes Legal Thinking Visible

Legal writing exposes process. Reasoning must appear on the page in a form another reader can easily follow. As a result, legal writing is often where misalignment becomes visible:

- doctrine understood but applied inaccurately

- research gathered but analysis underdeveloped

- accuracy without prioritization or vice versa

- volume mistaken for persuasion

Strong writing is not the result of endless revision or excessive length. It emerges from clear thinking, disciplined structure, and deliberate editing. In both law school and practice, page limits are real. Precision is therefore necessary, not a preference. The ability to synthesize, prioritize, and communicate exactly what must be said—without excess—is what distinguishes effective legal writing from mere verbosity.

Oral Advocacy Is Written Logic Spoken Under Time Pressure

Oral advocacy is often mistaken for confidence or performance. In reality, it is written analysis compressed into real time. Oral advocacy is evaluated on:

- responsiveness to the question asked

- command of the governing rule

- prioritization under interruption

- judgment about what to concede and what to defend

Fluency without substance is exposed quickly. Substance without structure collapses under questioning.

The strongest advocates are *not* the most theatrical. They are the most disciplined in execution.

MASTER YOUR COGNITIVE REALITY

Students who attempt to apply sound strategies through systems that do not fit how they process information under pressure are likely to remain inefficient. Cognitive processing must be functional to determine:

- how quickly confusion converts into clarity

- how long focus can be sustained before fatigue sets in

- whether repetition strengthens understanding or dulls it

- which study behaviors restore confidence versus erode it

Common Processing Tendencies Under Constraint

- Some students perform best when they can extract rules early and structure analysis before application. These students require analytical depth before confidence forms.

- Others process better when they articulate material early through explanation or writing before extended review. These students require verbal synthesis before confidence forms.

- Some perform best when they establish the overall framework before engaging specific rules. These students require structural orientation before details make sense.

- Others are sequential executors. They gain confidence through ordered steps and predictable routines. Open-ended study plans create drift. These students benefit from checklists, fixed sequences, and repeatable workflows.

- Some perform best when they engage application early through hypotheticals or exam-style problems. These students require contextual relevance before understanding feels stable. Abstract review without visible stakes leads to disengagement and shallow retention.

Each tendency has its own strengths along its failure modes. Under pressure, strengths can invert. For example:

- Depth-oriented students may over-analyze

- Articulators may mistake explanation for mastery

- Structure-first learners may delay engagement with detail

- Sequential executors may cling to routines that no longer fit evolving demands

- Context-driven learners may neglect foundational understanding

Finding the fit your processing tendency requires more than knowing how you prefer to study. It requires you to recognize when your default tendencies begin to cost you time or accuracy.

That is why you need to design guardrails around your strengths. Effective systems reduce friction and convert effort into results predictably. Under constraint, the question is not how you can learn. It is how you execute with the least waste of time and energy.

This may mean:

- starting with practice problems instead of outlining

- writing short synthesis memos instead of rereading

- studying in shorter focused intervals

- using structured repetition instead of constant variation

None of these choices are inherently superior. They work only when they fit you and your reality.

MASTER WHAT YOU CAN CONTROL

Law school contains many variables you cannot control. You cannot control:

- how difficult an exam will be

- how other students will perform

- where the curve will fall

- unexpected disruptions in life

Energy spent on uncontrollable variables is energy removed from execution. Constraint-driven students must redirect that energy. Identify what *is* within your control and master it.

For example, you *can* likely control:

- how clearly you structure your analysis

- how well you understand governing rules

- how early you seek clarification

- how consistently you practice under timed conditions

- how you manage sleep, preparation, and follow-through

- how professionally you communicate

In a word, mastery of controllables reduces friction. For example:

- Organizing materials weekly prevents last-minute scrambling

- Preparing questions before office hours clarifies issues quickly

- Editing for clarity preserves points

- Planning around predictable disruptions prevents reactive panic

None of these actions guarantee an A. However, all of them increase stability. Consistent control of preparation is what ultimately shifts outcomes.

3.   VISIT THE OFFICE OF ACADEMIC SUPPORT

Across U.S. law schools, what is commonly referred to as the Office of Academic Support appears under a range of functionally equivalent labels such as Academic Success, Student Success, Academic Achievement, Academic Excellence, or Bar Support, depending on how the institution frames the service. Many students misunderstand its purpose and assume it exists primarily for those who are struggling. As a result, they delay leveraging it or avoiding it altogether. This is a mistake. Academic support is not remedial per se. It is *institutional intelligence.*

This office exists to identify and correct ineffective patterns while reinforcing effective ones: how exams are written, how answers are graded, where students consistently lose points, which subjects they struggle with, which weeks are particularly intense, which study habits are unproductive or waste time, and what separates strong performance from average work.

Used Early, Academic Support Functions as an Early-Warning System Rather Than a Safety Net

While services vary by institution, academic support offices commonly provide insight into:

- exam structure and timing

- common analytical errors

- effective outlining and issue-spotting methods

- professor or course-specific testing trends

- performance benchmarks for strong answers

This institution-specific information is rarely available through common readings. It reflects institutional memory and *repeated* exposure to outcomes over time.

When to Use Academic Support

The optimal time to engage Academic Support is *before* you feel behind. Early engagement allows you to:

- get early tutoring to the extent possible

- validate whether your study approach aligns with expectations

- correct inefficiencies before they compound

- identify weaknesses while there is still time to adjust

- reduce anxiety by replacing guesswork with clarity

While seeking help *early* is ideal, seeking help at *any* point is better than seeking none at all. If you are already struggling, academic support will help you diagnose problems, adjust strategy, and prevent further damage.

Waiting until after one receives poor exam results or low grades limits what Academic Support can do. At that stage, the focus shifts from prevention to repair. The earlier you engage, the more options remain available. However, even late intervention is preferable to continuing without guidance.

Why This Matters for Non-Traditional Students

High-performing students ask questions. They seek feedback. They course-correct early. This is true in law school and in every evaluative environment where outcomes matter. Non-traditional students cannot afford to believe that support is only for those who are failing. In reality, it is what prevents failure in the first place.

Academic failure unfolds in stages: early confusion, missed signals, declining performance, academic warning, probation, and, eventually, dismissal or forced withdrawal. By the time probation is imposed, options are already limited. By the time dismissal is considered, correction is no longer the goal.

Seeking help before you need it is not insecurity. It is loss prevention.

Non-traditional students cannot absorb extended periods of inefficiency or misdirected effort. Early correction preserves margin; delayed correction consumes it. Academic Support helps you:

- protect limited resources

- identify errors before they escalate

- stabilize performance prior to formal intervention

- reduce reliance on last-minute recovery strategies

- evaluate whether there are actual reasons to worry in the first place

Leveraging academic support is not an admission of weakness. It is recognition that evaluative systems reward those who learn how they operate—and intervene before consequences harden.

4.   WHAT TO DO AFTER YOUR FIRST DISAPPOINTING RESULT

When your first grades or feedback arrive and they are lower than expected, do not spiral. A disappointing result is not a verdict on your ability, intelligence, or future performance. It is *information.*

Your first task is to dissociate academic worth from self-worth. Pause before interpreting. Do not assign meaning immediately. One assessment reflects one moment in time that was evaluated under specific criteria. It does not define you. It is actually better to fail early and fast and get it out of the way, so there is more time left in the journey for improvement.

Consider "Failure" as Data

Within the Constraint-Driven Method™, failure is not treated as feedback on ability or effort. It is treated as information about system design. In high-stakes environments, breakdowns usually occur because capacity was exceeded, sequencing was premature, or effort was applied where evaluative signal was low.

When results disappoint, the correct response is not escalation. It is diagnosis. This distinction matters. High-performing non-traditional students are particularly susceptible to misinterpreting failure as a personal deficiency. In reality, failure more often reflects a system that no longer fits current conditions.

The Method therefore requires that disappointing outcomes be examined through a structural lens.

Failure that is interpreted correctly improves performance. Failure that is moralized depletes it. Adjustment—not self-judgment—is the appropriate response.

Separate Outcome from Method

Ask yourself: *"What did I do to prepare, and how was my performance evaluated?"*

Early disappointments stem from predictable mismatches including:

- studying doctrine without practicing application

- outlining without writing timed answers

- reading more instead of practicing exams

- preparing generally rather than preparing for a particular professor

The issue is rarely that you "didn't work hard enough." More often, you worked hard on the wrong inputs. Before the next assessment cycle:

- attend office hours with your professors

- ask them how answers are evaluated in that specific class

- confirm what earns points and what does not

Do not feel so discouraged that you postpone corrective action.

Ask Questions Strategically

Strategic questions improve performance. Too often, students ask questions like:

"What will be on the midterm?"

"Will the final exam cover what was on the midterm?"

Others drift into hypothetical debates—*"If I were the judge, I would have ruled differently"*—or offer unsolicited critiques that a case is subjective or unfair.

Some even argue back and forth with professors they are meant to learn from, just for the sake of arguing. They misunderstand the role of the evaluator. Arguing with the person who defines the standards and assigns the grades does not improve performance. You must ask questions strategically by:

- Being specific. Vague questions produce vague answers. Identify and address your precise point of uncertainty.

- Being timely. Ask before the exam cycle.

- Being professional. Frame questions as an effort to meet expectations, not as a request for reassurance.

Productive questions go along the line of:

- "How can my approach become consistent with how exams are graded in this course?"

- "Where do students most commonly lose points on this type of exam or these particular issues?"

- "What distinguishes a strong answer from an average one?"

Ask questions that signal seriousness, preparation, and yield *actionable* guidance.

Adjust One Variable at a Time

Resist the urge to overhaul everything. Keep what worked. Only change what did not. Evaluate how you (1) practice, (2) apply rules, and (3) structure answers. Strategic adjustment is targeted, not frantic.

Diagnose, Do not Self-Indict

The feeling of failure is common in law school. What distinguishes high performers is not avoiding failure but responding to it correctly when it happens. After a disappointing result, many students ask:

"Am I smart enough?"

"Do I belong here?"

"Is law school for me?"

These questions feel natural, but they are strategically useless. The correct response must be diagnostic:

- What did I do or fail to do that produced this outcome?

- Which assumptions turned out to be inaccurate?

- What does this result teach me about this professor, this course, or the curve?

Failure is feedback about misalignment. Until you extract that information, the failure (or the opportunity to improve) is wasted. Improvement is not always linear. Some adjustments produce quick gains; others take time to show results.

After you diagnose: write down what you learned, adjust deliberately, and return to execution.

Guard Your Mind

Shame distorts judgment. Panic accelerates bad decisions. You must stay calm long enough to learn. It will allow you to assess results without spiraling into paralysis or comparison.

5.   STRATEGIC LOAD REDUCTION

Give yourself permission to redesign the path without abandoning the goal. Sometimes, the best strategy is to lighten the load.

When performance breaks down, the question is not whether someone is capable or hardworking, but rather whether the system they are operating within has become unsustainable. Continuing under conditions that cannot be sustained usually leads to deeper academic and personal consequences. Exhaustion increases, comprehension declines, and confidence erodes.

A controlled reduction in load can allow operating conditions to stabilize and protect long-term trajectory, making it possible to return stronger once capacity is restored.

Sometimes the most strategic move may be to pause long enough to rebuild the system.

Reducing the Load Does Not Mean Abandoning the Goal

One of the most common reasons systems fail is simple: the load exceeds the capacity available to carry it. Working harder does not create more time. Motivation does not replace sleep, focus, or emotional stability. If the load remains the same while capacity declines, the system eventually collapses.

Reducing the load does not necessarily mean abandoning the goal of becoming a lawyer. It often means adjusting the path. A student who withdraws from a course may retake it later under stronger conditions. A student who takes a temporary leave may return with restored focus and energy. A student who reduces their academic pace may ultimately perform better than one who tries to carry an unsustainable workload.

Progress is not measured by speed alone. For non-traditional students, pacing is strategic.

Even institutions expect structural adjustment; that is why they provide mechanisms such as course withdrawals, leaves of absence, deferments, and accommodations. The key is to make these decisions deliberately, based on reality rather than pride or fear.

When the Path Changes

There is another possibility that must be addressed honestly. Sometimes the issue is not temporary capacity. Sometimes the realization is that law itself may not be the right path.

This realization can be difficult, especially after investing time, effort, and financial resources. Students may feel pressure to continue because of expectations from family, institutions, or themselves.

But there is no value in forcing a life path that does not fit. If, after careful reflection, you conclude that the legal profession is not aligned with your interests, values, or long-term goals, there is no shame in choosing a different direction.

Changing course is not failure.

People perform best in environments that match their abilities and motivations. Judging a fish by its ability to climb a tree makes it appear incapable, even though it was designed to swim.

Recognizing where you do not belong and acting accordingly is a sign of maturity.

Protecting the Long-Term Path

Strategic load reduction is not about lowering standards. It is about protecting the long-term path. The Constraint-Driven Method™ requires that reality be incorporated into design.

- Sometimes the right move is to push forward under pressure

- Sometimes the right move is to rebuild the foundation

- Sometimes the right move is to choose a different path entirely

What matters is that the decision is made deliberately and with *clarity*.

This principle strengthens the Constraint-Driven Method™ by preventing avoidable academic loss through seeking help early.

11

FILTER OUT NOISE

Performance under constraint requires selective attention. When time, energy, and cognitive bandwidth are limited, every input competing for attention must justify its presence. Much of what surrounds law students like advice, commentary, and perceived expectations, functions as noise rather than signal. Non-traditional students must identify and filter those inputs, so effort remains aligned with performance.

---

1. UNDERSTAND WHOSE OPINION ACTUALLY MATTERS

One of the fastest ways law students lose ground is by listening to too many voices. Law school is loud. Opinions circulate constantly in the form of study group advice, online forums, group chats, upper-class anecdotes, social media commentary, and well-meaning peers offering strategies that worked *for them*. Much of this information is not malicious. Some of it can even be accurate. But most of it is irrelevant. Not all noise is informational; some of it is simply distraction. Noise is not defined by whether advice is true. Noise is defined by whether advice *affects* outcomes.

Noise Is Best Understood as Signal Interference

Think of law school like a radio spectrum. At any given moment, countless signals are broadcasting simultaneously. Opinions, strategies, anxieties, rumors, and predictions are constant. However, what you hear depends entirely on where you tune the dial.

Most students assume noise comes from volume. It does not. It comes from *misalignment*. When you tune into every frequency at once, the result is distortion, not information. Filtering noise is about choosing which signals deserve access to your attention.

Professors, grading rubrics, past exams, and official academic guidance operate on clear, stable frequencies. Peer commentary often does not. It is fragmented, incomplete, and influenced by incentives you may *not* share.

Your performance improves when you stop scanning the spectrum and commit to the channels that actually carry a signal. Tuning into the right frequency is the key.

Think of Law School Like a YouTube Algorithm

At any given moment, millions of videos are being uploaded. The feed never stops. What you see is not "what's out there." It is what you have trained the system to surface.

If you click on stress, you get more stress. If you click on unfiltered peer speculation, you get endless opinion. If you chase novelty, the algorithm rewards you with distraction. But when you consistently engage with authoritative, outcome-aligned content, the feed changes.

Law school works the same way.

You are surrounded by information, but information is not a signal. A signal is what directly affects evaluation and outcomes. Professors, grading criteria, institutional rules, and repeatable patterns drive results. Everything else is content. High-performing students do not consume more information. They curate their inputs. They "train the algorithm" of their attention to surface:

- evaluator priorities

- tested issues

- proven strategies

- reliable feedback

Grades In Law School Are Not Crowdsourced

Grades in law school are not negotiated. They are not determined by consensus. They are controlled by a small number of people, often *one*. Understanding this is not cynical. It is clarifying. Every course has an evaluator. That evaluator decides:

- what constitutes a strong answer

- how analysis is rewarded

- which mistakes cost the most points

- how performance is ranked

No amount of peer agreement overrides that reality.

When students give equal weight to all opinions, they dilute their focus. When non-traditional students do this, the cost is higher because time and energy are already constrained.

Why Noise Is Especially Dangerous for Non-Traditional Students

Newborn babies sleep through white noise because it dulls awareness. Law school has its own version. Constant chatter, opinions, and performative confidence can lull you into complacency if you let it. Traditional students often have margin. They can experiment, discard approaches, and recalibrate later. Non-traditional students rarely have the luxury to deal with the confusion and lost efficiency that noise creates:

- unnecessary doubt

- misdirected effort

- constant strategy switching

- emotional volatility

Filtering noise is not about being dismissive. It is about protecting limited resources.

Recognize and Listen to the Voices That Matter

In most law school settings, authoritative voices fall into a small set of categories:

- professors and exam authors

- academic support professionals

- institutional administrators with discretion

- official course materials and policies

These are the voices that shape outcomes. They are the ones worth prioritizing. Everyone else may be supportive, insightful, or well-intentioned—but they are not determinative.

2. BEWARE OF PEER CALIBRATION

Many students rely heavily on peers to assess whether they are "on track." This is risky because peers:

- are subject to the same uncertainty you are

- may be overconfident or underprepared

- may succeed or fail for reasons unrelated to strategy

- do not grade your exams

Peer Behavior Is Not Always a Reliable Metric

Peer behavior is not a reliable metric for performance. Law students observe one another constantly—who speaks in class, who appears confident, who studies late, who claims to understand the material—and often infer meaning from these signals. Most of those inferences are wrong. Visibility is not accuracy. Confidence is not competence. Shared habits do not reflect grading standards.

Evaluative systems reward alignment with criteria, not conformity with peers. Students who calibrate their effort based on what classmates appear to be doing risk optimizing for the wrong signals. High performance comes from understanding how evaluation works, not from mirroring peer behavior.

Peer calibration is further compromised by unreliable reporting. Some students exaggerate their performance. Others selectively disclose information. A few misrepresent results entirely. This is not always malicious; it is often driven by insecurity or self-protection. Regardless of motive, the data is distorted and unsuitable for decision-making.

Distortion intensifies after exams. Once an exam is submitted, the outcome is fixed. Rehashing questions, comparing answers, or speculating about grading does not improve performance. It generates anxiety without producing actionable insight. Meaningful assessment begins only after results are released. Until then, discussion is noise.

Be Cautious of Labels

Labels attract stereotypes, and stereotypes can shape behavior. Once you accept a label, you begin to perform it. Get called a "coaster," and suddenly you second-guess raising your hand, asking a question, or engaging fully despite doing exactly what you are supposed to do.

The same is true of cultural slogans like "Cs get degrees." Ironically, it is often repeated by high-performing students who have no intention of getting Cs. Do not mistake casual rhetoric for a viable strategy.

Guard your mind with diligence. Develop the discipline of hearing strategically and ignoring what does not serve you well.

Do not follow peers blindly. If they are not encouraging disciplined execution, their input should be limited—or filtered out entirely. This does not mean isolating yourself. It means understanding the limits of peer feedback.

Peers are useful for:

- shared accountability

- emotional support

- collaborative practice

They are not reliable arbiters of evaluative standards.

Noise Often Disguises Itself as Diligence

Noise feels productive until it is not. Listening to multiple strategies can feel like thoroughness. Gathering many opinions can feel like preparation. But excessive input without hierarchy leads to paralysis. Constraint-driven students must ask:

- Who controls the outcome?

- What evidence supports this advice?

- Does this align with what evaluators reward?

If the answer is unclear, the advice is noise.

This principle strengthens the Constraint-Driven Method™ by protecting limited time and energy from misalignment, ensuring execution remains anchored to the voices and standards that actually determine outcomes.

12

Repeat What Works for You

As non-traditional students begin to see improvement, many fall into what I call the "comparative distortion" trap. In the search for a better strategy or in response to what others appear to be doing, they abandon the very approaches that have produced results. Clearer expectations, stronger exam performance, or a more effective outline are treated as provisional rather than systems to be stabilized. Instead of consolidating what works, students chase constant refinement, assuming progress requires perpetual innovation. It does not. Progress must come from disciplined repetition.

---

1.   Why Reinvention Is a Hidden Risk

Law school rewards consistency more than creativity. Exams are graded against stable criteria. Evaluators value clarity, structure, and accurate application of the law to the facts, not novelty. Reinvention introduces unnecessary risk:

- it resets learning curves

- it consumes time and energy

- it disrupts momentum

- it increases variability in performance

For non-traditional students, variability can be dangerous because time and energy are limited. Predictability is thus an advantage. Repeating what works is how you protect that advantage.

Less Can Be more

Students often assume that success requires adding more tools: more supplements, more methods, more resources. In reality, high performance usually improves by *removing* what does not work and *refining* what does. Once you identify a strategy that produces results for you:

- keep the core structure

- reduce unnecessary additions

- focus on execution quality

Refinement beats replacement.

2. WHAT "WORKS" MUST BE DEFINED BY OUTCOMES

Repeating what works requires clarity about what success looks like.

"Working" does *not* mean:

- feeling productive

- studying longer

- matching peers' habits

"Working" means:

- reduced confusion

- improved efficiency

- clearer feedback from evaluators

- higher scores over time

Outcomes—not effort—determine what should be repeated.

Adapt Without Abandoning

Repeating what works does not mean rigidly applying the same approach everywhere. Courses differ. Professors differ. Formats differ. While the structure remains, the application must adapt by:

- using the same outlining framework across courses, adjusted for content

- applying the same exam strategy while tailoring analysis to each course and/or professor

- preserving study rhythms while adjusting timing

The mistake is not adaptation. The mistake is discarding a proven system entirely.

3. REPETITION CREATES RELIABILITY

Over time, repetition does something more important than improvement: it creates reliability.

Reliable students:

- know what to do when pressure rises

- do not panic after setbacks

- execute without constant recalibration

- trust their process

Reliability is not glamorous. It is powerful. Under constraint, reliability allows performance to continue even when circumstances are imperfect.

Why This Principle Matters More Over Time

Early in law school, experimentation is unavoidable. You are learning the system. But once you crack the code—even partially—progress accelerates when you stop experimenting and start operationalizing.

Many students plateau not because they stop working, but because they keep changing strategies instead of letting one appreciate over time.

This principle strengthens the Constraint-Driven Method™ by stabilizing execution and allowing effective strategies to compound, reducing variability, and preserving momentum under real-world constraints.

OPERATIONAL SUMMARY: PART III

This part requires disciplined execution.

You are expected to stop reacting to volume, urgency, and comparison, and instead operate from systems that create buffer, filter noise, and convert effort into reliable outcomes. You must design execution around reality, not preference or imitation.

Before moving forward, you should have at least one execution system that is repeatable, aligned with how you process information under constraint, and capable of producing consistent results without continual reinvention.

PART IV — RELATIONAL & INSTITUTIONAL LEVERAGE

"Where you stand depends on where you sit."
— **Rufus Mile**

13

STUDY AND EMULATE SUCCESS WHERE YOU ARE

Success in law school rarely requires reinventing the process. In nearly every institution, there are students who have already identified what works within that specific environment. Rather than guessing or relying on generic advice, you should observe, study, and emulate the patterns of success already present around your institution.

---

1.   SUCCESS LEAVES CLUES

Success does leave clues. You must nevertheless look in the *right* place(s) to find them.

Many law students seek guidance by consuming broad, generic success stories: top graduates, high-ranking students, and widely shared narratives of academic excellence. These accounts are often credible. The outcomes are real. The discipline is evident.

The problem is not that these examples are wrong. The problem is that they are frequently context blind.

Why Generic Success Has Limits

Generic success stories emphasize universal principles, but they often feature students who entered law school straight from college with few obligations and full control over their time, making them a poor reference point for non-traditional students.

What works in theory can fail in practice because principles depend on context. For example, real estate may be a sound investment, but buying property in a war-torn area with ongoing combat turns a good principle into a bad decision. Instead of asking: *"Who is the most successful?"* Reframe it as: *"Who is successful under conditions similar to mine?"*

Equally important, you must define what success means for you. Success does not look the same for everyone. For some students, it means finishing in the top 10 percent of the class. For others, it means graduating on an accelerated timeline, or obtaining an early job offer.

Your definition of success determines who you should learn from and what you should copy.

The goal is not to copy someone else's outcome. The goal is to learn from people whose strategies actually fit your life—and adapt them deliberately to your own environment and definition of success.

Local Success Is the Most Actionable Success

Although the legal world is global and advice from top-tier schools is widely accessible, only success at the law school you attend reveals answers to questions generic advice can never provide. For example:

- How does *this* professor grade?

- Which outlines actually work *here*?

- How much writing versus memorization does *this* exam reward?

- What does "doing well" look like in *this* academic culture?

At your law school, intentionally study success stories and seek to be connected with individuals who:

- Attended the *same* school

- Took classes with the *same* professors

- Lived in the *same* region

- Balanced *comparable* personal obligations

They do not need to be Ivy League celebrities. They do not need to have a story that has gone viral. But they are proof that success is possible where you stand. Likewise, you must closely pay attention to:

- How top students structure their weeks

- When they study, not just how long

- How they handle burnout

- Which resources they utilize and which ones they ignore entirely

You will discover that high performers are *very* selective. They do not do everything. They focus on what matters and repeat it consistently.

2.   FAILURE IS PREDICTABLE

Failure in law school is rarely mysterious. It follows patterns as well. As you are studying success stories, study failure stories also, so you know what *not* to do.

There are highly qualified individuals who are sent to academic probation at the end of their 1L year. Most students who underperform are not less intelligent, less motivated, or less capable. They fail for structural reasons: they prepare in ways that are misaligned with how success is evaluated.

This predictability is uncomfortable because it strips failure of its drama. It is easier to believe that poor outcomes are random, unfair, or personal than to accept that they are often the foreseeable result of repeatable *choices*.

For example:

- Students who do not study past exams struggle on exam day

- Students who do not practice under exam conditions do not finish on time on exam day

- Students who ignore professor feedback miss grading priorities

- Students who do not take class hypotheticals seriously miss what could appear on the final exam

- Students who rely on generalized study advice instead of course-specific signals are surprised by results they should have anticipated.

None of this is accidental.

Law school is not designed to reward effort evenly. It rewards specific behaviors, and those behaviors can be *observed, tracked, and replicated*. When students study in isolation without reference to exemplars of success they increase the likelihood of predictable failure.

This is why emulation matters.

High-performing students leave clues: their outlines mirror the structure of top exams, their rule statements track professor language, and their time allocation reflects grading weight. If you ignore those signals, it is likely that you will not be a high-performing student because outcomes follow patterns.

Studying to emulate success is also about knowing where others have failed and avoiding their mistakes. It is about recognizing that excellence leaves a trail and choosing not to walk past it.

3.   HOW TO STUDY SUCCESS WHERE YOU ARE

Studying success effectively requires disciplined observation, selective imitation, and continuous calibration to the environment in which performance is evaluated. You must:

Identify three to five individuals one step ahead of you. Focus on students who have recently performed well under conditions materially similar to your own. Relevance matters more than prestige; success achieved with different constraints is not instructive.

Observe before asking questions. Watch how these students allocate time, what they consistently prioritize, and what they intentionally avoid. Look for patterns across behavior and choices rather than isolated habits or anecdotes.

Extract principles, not personalities. Do not copy routines, schedules, or study aesthetics. Reverse-engineer the underlying decisions that produce results in your institutional environment.

Ask questions that reveal structure, not reassurance. Direct questions to individuals who understand grading mechanics, course expectations, and evaluation norms. Focus on how performance is assessed, not how stress is managed.

Seek mentorship that provides institutional access. Formal or informal mentors shorten the learning curve by clarifying which signals matter, which rules are rigid, and where flexibility exists.

Test selectively and refine continuously. Apply strategies within your own constraints, monitor outcomes, and adjust based on evidence. Consistency and reliability matter more than intensity.

Discard what does not translate. Retain what produces results under your conditions and abandon what does not.

The quiet overlooked advantage to studying success where you are is that *it removes doubt*. When someone with similar or worse constraints succeeds in the same environment, excuses lose power. It becomes easier to trust the process and stay the course.

This principle strengthens the Constraint-Driven Method™ by directing effort toward strategies that work in your actual environment.

14

BUILD YOUR LAW SCHOOL VILLAGE

No one succeeds in law school *alone*—some people are just better at hiding their village. The myth of the lone, hyper-disciplined law student is exactly that: a myth. You will soon find out that behind nearly every high performer is an informal network of people who share notes, clarify rules, flag traps, offer encouragement, and provide reality checks when pressure distorts judgment.

---

1. WHY A LAW SCHOOL VILLAGE IS NOT OPTIONAL

A law school village is a network of people who provide academic or emotional support, whether within or outside the law school.

Law school villages can form by chance through early friendships or assigned groups, or they can be built intentionally. Either way, a village is not optional because isolation is costly.

A village is not about dependency; it is about perspective. Different people notice different things: how a professor frames questions, how doctrine actually shows up on exams, or how to make the material usable. Working with others reduces blind spots and prevents avoidable mistakes.

For students with constraints, collaboration matters but not everyone belongs in the same role. Priority should be given to people with similar goals, similar constraints, or a shared commitment to doing the work. You must become intentional about building relationships as needed to stay effective.

Each group you join must serve a purpose. The key is knowing which group to turn to and when.

Every Effective Village Has Roles

In groups of non-traditional law students, certain functions often emerge naturally as people contribute according to their strengths and experiences:

- *The Clarifier*: helps translate complex concepts into clear explanations when the material becomes difficult to grasp or confusion arises.

- *The Outliner*: organizes doctrine into structured frameworks that make the material easier to review and recall.

- *The Examiner*: challenges the group with questions, hypotheticals, and practice problems to test real understanding before exams.

- *The Archivist*: keeps track of notes, resources, and insights so the group's knowledge compounds over time.

- *The Encourager*: offers perspective and support during demanding periods when outside responsibilities compete with study.

- *The Motivator*: pushes the group to maintain discipline, consistency, and forward momentum when fatigue, work, or family obligations threaten consistency.

You do not need to be everything. You need to know where you add value and where others do. Villages thrive when members contribute from strength rather than compete from insecurity.

2.   WHAT A LAW SCHOOL VILLAGE SHOULD NOT BE

Your village should not become a space for constant complaining, comparison, gossip, or resistance. Clear boundaries matter. Not every group is healthy, and not every discussion is productive.

Protect Your Village by Limiting Exposure to Chronic Complaining

Law students are exceptionally good at identifying what feels unfair, inefficient, or unreasonable. Complaining is very common. However, law school is not a democracy. You do not vote on grading curves, exam formats, or institutional norms. These norms exist independent of individual preference. Expending energy resisting them does not alter outcomes; it only diverts attention from performance.

The more productive approach is adaptation. When you travel between systems, you do not argue with the rules you learn them. If you drive in a country where traffic flows on the opposite side of the road, the rule is not wrong simply because it differs from what you know. It is operative. Safe passage depends on understanding and complying with it.

Law school functions the same way. The rules may not be intuitive, familiar, or personally designed for you but they govern evaluation all the same. Strategic performance begins by recognizing which rules apply and adjusting accordingly.

Protect Your Village by Limiting Exposure to Comparison-Driven Anxiety

Unmanaged comparison is one of the fastest ways to destabilize a law school village. The moment you begin measuring yourself against another student's pace, grades, or outward confidence, attention shifts away from your own execution. Law students are not moving along a single track. One student's success does not diminish yours, and another's struggle does not forecast your outcome.

Progress in law school is not synchronized. Some students perform well early. Others improve later. What matters is not where someone else appears to be, but whether *your* understanding, judgment, and execution are improving over time.

A healthy law school village depends on members remaining grounded in their own trajectory. Growth should be assessed against who you were last week or last assessment, not against who someone else appears to be today.

Unchecked comparison often produces impostor syndrome. It usually begins subtly: another student speaks confidently, shares a success, or seems certain; this leads to uncertainty in yourself, which is then misread as deficiency. That inference is inaccurate. Confidence is not a reliable proxy for competence, particularly in environments with delayed and opaque feedback.

Admission to law school is itself a gatekeeping decision. Committees evaluate records, context, and capacity before extending an offer. That determination reflects institutional judgment, not chance. It should not be overridden by peer comparison or momentary self-doubt.

Protect Your Village by Limiting Exposure to Gossip Disguised as Concern

Academic gossip undermines excellence. It often disguises itself as information-sharing, but it rarely improves performance.

Speculating about grades, ranking classmates, or dissecting perceived favoritism should be a hard no. High-performing villages trade in *clarity*, not speculation.

If a conversation does not improve understanding, preparation, or morale, it does not belong in your village. Your village should reduce friction, not increase it.

Protect Your Village by Not Prejudging Classmates

Prejudging classmates is a common and costly mistake. Some students act as though they are above others or avoid associating with certain people based on assumptions about ability, background, or ambition. That posture is misguided.

Every student in your class earned a place in law school. More importantly, law school is not a closed system. The classmates around you today will become colleagues, referral sources, supervisors, clients, and decision-makers tomorrow. Relationships formed during law school often extend well beyond graduation.

Building a strong village requires openness beyond surface impressions or labels. Be willing to engage broadly, while remaining intentional about alignment. As long as your academic goals and values are compatible, proximity is not a risk.

This principle strengthens the Constraint-Driven Method™ by replacing resistance, comparison, and wasted effort with humility, adaptation, and collaborative efficiency.

15

Know Your Institutional Gatekeepers

Institutional and student success are not competing interests. Law schools are evaluated on outcomes—retention, passing the bar, employment, and long-term reputation. Students who perform well strengthen the institution; students who disengage or fail impose real costs, even when those costs are diffuse or delayed.

For this reason, engaging institutional resources is not asking for special treatment. It is participating responsibly in a system designed to produce successful graduates. Professors, administrators, and support office staff are structural actors who favor student success when engagement is timely, informed, and professional.

Constraint-driven students must collaborate openly with institutional gatekeepers not out of dependence, but out of strategy. Doing so advances both individual performance and institutional outcomes.

---

1.   Engage Professors

Every institution has gatekeepers: individuals who shape outcomes, interpret standards, and decide what excellence looks like within that system. In law school, professors are not only educators; they are evaluators, and their role in your success is both formal and decisive.

For that reason, professors should be engaged deliberately as evaluators and educators rather than treated as abstractions to be avoided, endured, or challenged without purpose.

Your task is not to impress professors in the abstract. It is to demonstrate competence as they define it. Engaging professors does not require excessive office-hour visits, performative participation, or artificial enthusiasm.

It means:

- Listening carefully to how they frame issues

- Noting what they emphasize repeatedly

- Observing how they reward structure, analysis, and clarity

- Asking targeted, prepared questions

Office Hours Are Intelligence Briefings

Office hours are not confessional spaces, therapy sessions, or remedial interventions. They are *intelligence briefings*. Their purpose is not visibility or reassurance, but precision. They are structured opportunities for alignment. When used correctly, office hours help you understand how performance is evaluated and how your preparation should be adjusted.

Effective use of office hours allows you to:

- clarify grading priorities

- test whether your analytical depth is sufficient

- confirm how exam structure is weighted

- identify common errors before they appear on assessments

- align preparation with the professor's grading lens

- resolve doctrinal misunderstandings

These meetings should be intentional and efficient. Arrive with specific questions grounded in your work. Leave with concrete guidance you can implement immediately.

Importantly, you do not need a fully formed question to benefit from office hours. You can still benefit by listening to other students' questions and to professors' spontaneous explanations or clarifications. These often reveal how material is framed, prioritized, and evaluated. Professors frequently disclose grading preferences, recurring mistakes, and analytical shortcuts in response to questions they did not anticipate. These insights are rarely repeated elsewhere.

Over time, patterns emerge. You will recognize which issues are emphasized, where precision matters more than breadth, and how evaluators allocate attention under grading pressure. This information directly informs exam preparation and reduces preventable error.

For non-traditional students especially, time and energy are finite resources. Office hours must therefore be treated as high-leverage interactions respectful of both your constraints and the professor's time. The objective is not validation. It is understanding. Different professors reward different competencies. Some emphasize:

- issue spotting over depth

- structure over originality

- precedent over policy

- clarity over volume

At the same time, professors operate within grading rubrics, time constraints, and institutional norms. Their feedback reflects not only personal preference, but institutional reality. Understanding this context allows you to interpret guidance accurately and apply it effectively.

Success depends on identifying what *each* evaluator values and aligning your execution accordingly. Effort that is not aligned with evaluation criteria does not yield results. The earlier you achieve alignment, the more efficiently every subsequent hour of study produces results.

Lastly, law school is not only academic training; it is professional conditioning. In practice, judges, partners, clients, and regulators will evaluate your work. Learning to read expectations, adapt execution, and deliver accordingly is what competence is about. Law school is where this skill is learned in a controlled environment.

2. BEYOND PROFESSORS: THE INSTITUTIONAL NETWORK

Successful students know who evaluates them, how evaluation happens, where discretion exists, and who holds institutional knowledge that never appears in a syllabus.

This is actionable insight.

Professors are not the only gatekeepers in law school. Law schools are complex institutions run by different key individuals. Many of them have access to information and opportunity.

As a non-traditional student, you stand to benefit from understanding (and engaging, with intention) the broader network of institutional gatekeepers, including:

- **The Dean of Students**, who oversees discretion, accommodations, and crisis response

- **The Dean of Academic Affairs**, who interprets academic policies, enforcement, and exceptions

- **The Dean of Career Services**, who clarifies how performance translates into opportunity

- **Admissions and Diversity, Equity, and Inclusion (DEI) offices,** which illuminate institutional priorities, pipelines, and support structures

These offices often hold information that students discover too late, after deadlines have passed, options have narrowed, or misunderstandings have solidified into consequences. Early engagement provides clarity and strategic advantage. Students who succeed do not guess how the system works, they learn it. They ask and confirm:

- what flexibility exists

- when discretion can be exercised

- how policies are actually applied

- and which steps prevent avoidable problems

Clarity allows students to align preparation, communication, and expectations with reality instead of assumptions.

Institutional Fluency Means Understanding That Respect Carries Across Roles

Front desk staff, administrative assistants, coordinators, and custodial staff often know how the school actually operates. They understand informal processes, how to facilitate access, and how students conduct themselves.

You rarely know who will be helpful, when, or how. Courtesy costs nothing and often provides insight that no handbook will give. Professionalism is not for show. It is part of how things get done.

For non-traditional students, engaging institutional gatekeepers helps ensure that time is spent on what matters, energy is directed toward the right people, and misunderstandings are addressed before they become problems.

Law school rewards those who understand the system they are operating in.

3.   ETHICAL BOUNDARIES OF LEVERAGE

The Constraint-Driven Method™ teaches strategic engagement with institutions and relationships. This requires a clear ethical boundary.

Leverage, as used in this book, does not mean manipulation. It does not involve misrepresentation, corner-cutting, or exploiting asymmetries of information. It is not transactional networking or performative visibility.

Leverage refers to the disciplined use of available structures—policies, relationships, and institutional pathways—to expand outcomes without increasing strain. It relies on clarity, preparation, and respect for institutional norms.

Strategic engagement is ethical precisely because it operates within the rules of the system rather than attempting to evade them. It prioritizes alignment over advantage and sustainability over short-term gain.

This principle strengthens the Constraint-Driven Method™ by replacing generalized effort with evaluator-specific strategy, ensuring that limited time and energy are directed toward what decision-makers actually reward.

OPERATIONAL SUMMARY: PART IV

This part requires intentional engagement with people and institutions.

You are expected to study success where you are, build relationships strategically, and understand how influence and access actually function within your law school environment. This is not about visibility or networking for its own sake. It is about leverage.

Before proceeding, you should be able to identify the individuals, structures, and relationships that meaningfully affect outcomes and engage them deliberately rather than opportunistically.

PART V — LIFE MANAGEMENT DURING LAW SCHOOL

"The key is not to prioritize what's on your schedule, but to schedule your priorities." — **Stephen Covey**

16

ANCHORS THAT HOLD UNDER PRESSURE

Pressure is inevitable in law school. Deadlines accumulate, exams compress decision-making, and uncertainty tests focus and confidence. Students who remain effective under these conditions rely on anchors—stable practices and reference points that keep performance aligned when pressure rises.

---

1. WHAT SUSTAINED YOU BEFORE LAW SCHOOL?

Pressure reveals what you are anchored to. Law school applies a specific kind of pressure. It is sustained, evaluative, and identity challenging. It does not simply test the ability to learn doctrine; it tests what remains stable when outcomes are uncertain and feedback is delayed.

What sustained you before law school is often what sustains you during law school. Pressure does not create character. It reveals foundations. Many students enter law school believing they must become someone else to succeed. They assume that what previously grounded them—faith, family, service, values, discipline, or purpose—must be suspended in order to endure institutional demands.

Law school does not require new anchors. It requires reliance on existing ones.

The form of an anchor varies. For some students, it is faith. For others, it may be family responsibility, moral conviction, service commitments, identity, or a clearly articulated purpose. The form differs, but the function does not. An anchor provides orientation when conditions are unstable. It establishes a reference point that does not fluctuate with grades, rankings, or external validation.

Anchors do not remove pressure. They place it in context.

When outcomes are uncertain and timelines feel opaque, a stable anchor allows sustained effort without emotional collapse. The same holds true when results fluctuate. An anchor allows you to separate performance from worth, and effort from identity. Pressure remains but it becomes navigable rather than destabilizing.

Law school will try to rename you. If you allow it, law school will attempt to reduce you to administrative labels:

- rank
- GPA
- participation
- "strong" or "weak" writer
- "top" or "average" student

These labels serve institutional functions. They are not identities. The danger is not that these labels exist. The danger is *allowing* them to replace who you are. When identity collapses into performance, pressure becomes unbearable.

When students lack an anchor, they measure themselves constantly against peers' study habits, grades, recognition, timelines. That cycle produces anxiety, resentment, and despair.

Anchors interrupt that cycle.

They remind you that your path is specific, your responsibilities are real, and your timing is not a failure simply because it differs from everyone else's. Success elsewhere does not diminish your own.

2.   A NECESSARY CAUTION ABOUT ANCHORS

Not everything that helps someone cope under pressure is an anchor worth keeping.

If what sustained you in the past involved practices that are immoral, illegal, or unethical, those practices will not serve you here. Law school amplifies consequences. Behaviors that numbed stress before can quietly erode judgment, reliability, and credibility.

The Constraint-Driven Method™ operates within three non-negotiables: *what is moral, what is ethical, and what is legal.*

Practices that impair cognition, distort decision-making, or create dependency are incompatible with this Method. That includes substance misuse—whether socially normalized or privately rationalized—as well as shortcuts that compromise integrity.

Do not rely on substance abuse to endure law school, not even such accepted stimulants as excessive caffeine. Endurance in this Method is not manufactured chemically or borrowed temporarily. It is built structurally.

This is not about moral superiority. It is about sustainability. Anything that undermines clarity, judgment, or professional character will eventually cost more than it gives, especially in the legal field.

Anchors should stabilize you, not dull you.
They should strengthen judgment, not compromise it.
They should carry you forward, not create liabilities you must later undo.

3. INTEGRITY MATTERS MORE UNDER PRESSURE

Pressure reveals priorities. Under sustained pressure, you may be tempted to take shortcuts not only academically, but ethically and relationally. This is where anchors matter. Anchors function as guardrails. They keep you from becoming someone you do not recognize in the process of trying to survive an institution. Success that requires sacrificing integrity is too costly.

Law school is a season, not a destination. It will test you but should not define you. If your values and identity are consumed by the process, even achievement will feel empty. When your values are preserved, graduation becomes a transition rather than a collapse.

You move forward intact.
You still work hard. You still aim high.
But you are no longer destabilized by every outcome.

This chapter strengthens the Constraint-Driven Method™ by stabilizing identity under pressure.

17

PARENTING WHILE IN LAW SCHOOL WITHOUT GUILT

Parenting while in law school is difficult. Because of that reality, parenting and law school are often framed as incompatible. That framing is not only inaccurate, but also damaging. The problem is not parenting. The problem is guilt. Guilt convinces capable students that they are failing two worlds at once, but the truth is parenting does not disqualify you from excellence.

1. YOU ARE NOT CHOOSING LAW SCHOOL OVER YOUR CHILDREN

Many students who are parents carry a quiet fear that success in law school comes at the expense of their relationship with their children. This fear is misplaced because you are not choosing law school over your children. You are choosing long-term stability and expanded opportunity

Children do not require constant availability. They require consistency, emotional safety, and reliability. Those needs can coexist with ambition when parenting and law school are approached intentionally.

The demands of parenting, however, are not uniform.

Newborns require a level of physical presence and support that is fundamentally different from the needs of toddlers, school-age children, teenagers, or adult children. Many students navigate pregnancy, childbirth, and early parenting during law school. I myself had a baby during my 3L year and had two under two when I started. It is taxing. It can feel impossible. But it is doable with support, planning, and realistic expectations.

This is not an encouragement to add avoidable strain. Do not read this and assume that timing does not matter. In fact, many will advise you that you should not even acquire a pet during law school.

Parenting during law school *requires* help. The absence of support changes the equation entirely. But parenting and law school can coexist when approached with clarity and the right tools.

2.   YOU MUST ABANDON FALSE METRICS

False metrics are measures that quietly produce guilt but have no reliable connection to healthy parenting. Students who are parents often judge themselves by:

- hours spent with children rather than quality of engagement

- perfect attendance at every school or extracurricular event

- never missing bedtime or daily routines

- being constantly available on demand

- avoiding childcare or outside help

- children's short-term dissatisfaction

- comparison to non-student parents with different schedules and resources

- maintaining identical routines year-round, regardless of academic cycles

- never appearing tired, stressed, or distracted

- children's immediate academic or behavioral outcomes during transition periods

These metrics are unattainable when you are going to law school because they:

- ignore context

- punish temporary imbalance

- reward optics over substance

- confuse presence with effectiveness

They assume that good parenting requires constant availability and visible perfection. In fact, effective parenting (especially under constraint) is measured by consistency, emotional safety, communication, and long-term stability.

Presence Is About Quality, Not Duration

Presence is often misunderstood as uninterrupted time. In reality, presence is measured by attentiveness, intentionality, and follow-through.

Short, focused interactions often matter more than extended periods of *distracted* availability. Children recognize when attention is divided. They also recognize reliability. You must prioritize *quality time* with your children over quantity.

Structure Reduces Guilt

Guilt thrives in chaos. Clear routines reduce emotional friction. When children know when you are working and when you are fully theirs, conflict decreases. When those boundaries are honored consistently, trust builds.

Structure does not mean rigidity. There will be weeks when law school demands more and moments when family must come first. Balance does not require symmetry. Reject the idea that every day must feel equal to be fair.

Create a Dedicated Study Signal

You will benefit from a clear, visible boundary that signals when study is in session. This does not require a separate office or ideal conditions. It just requires consistency and meaning.

A dedicated study space functions as a signal to everyone in the household. When you are there, you are working. When you leave it, you are available again.

Children learn these signals quickly.

I noticed that my children would approach with a question, pause when they saw me reading or studying, and then say, "Never mind." That response did not come from fear or distance. It came from understanding. When boundaries are clear and predictable, children respect them. This kind of signal reduces interruptions without requiring constant explanation. It also removes guilt. You are not ignoring your children; you are honoring a defined work period that you will exit in due time.

Dedicated space is not about isolation.

When children know when they *can* access you and when they *cannot*, conflict decreases and trust increases. Law school demands focus. A visible study signal protects that focus while preserving the relationship on the other side of the boundary.

Explain the Demands of Law School to Your Children

Children cope better with change when they understand *why* the change is happening. Law school requires time, focus, and sustained attention. Failing to acknowledge the truth does not safeguard children; instead, it places the responsibility on them to understand absence independently.

You do not need to burden children with adult stress, but you should give them a clear, age-appropriate understanding of what law school requires and what it means for family time. When expectations are named, disappointment is less likely to become resentment.

There will be moments when your children feel the cost of your commitment. Some routines will change. Your presence will sometimes be reduced. These moments are real, and they should be acknowledged. What matters is clarity: your pursuit of law school does not signal withdrawal from the relationship itself.

As a parent, your task is to frame your time in law school accurately. That means explaining that:

- law school is temporary

- certain seasons require concentrated focus

- your commitment has a purpose

- your relationship with them remains secure

When children understand the framework, they are less likely to interpret busyness as rejection and more likely to experience it as part of a shared, time-bound effort.

Children Learn from What They Observe

Through your effort, they see:

- perseverance

- discipline

- sacrifice with purpose

- delayed gratification

These lessons endure longer than any missed bedtime or rescheduled activity.

Invite Participation Where Appropriate

Children do not only respond to absence or presence; they respond to meaning. Where appropriate, allowing children to observe or participate in aspects of law school can reduce distance and demystify the work.

When possible, children can engage in age-appropriate discussions about argument and reasoning. As they practice explaining positions, asking questions, and defending ideas, law school will become less abstract and less threatening.

Equally important, let them be present at the outcome. They should attend the graduation ceremony and share in the milestone of passing the bar. That way, they will understand that the effort had direction and the sacrifice led somewhere concrete.

Pursuing excellence is possible while parenting. When handled responsibly, it models how to commit to demanding goals with intention—how sacrifice is contextualized, how effort is sustained, and how difficult seasons conclude.

Law school is temporary. The habits and examples your children absorb are not.

A Note on Single Parenting

Single parenting during law school introduces a different magnitude of constraint. There may be no partner to absorb overflow, no default backup when schedules collide, and little margin for error. Time scarcity is sharper.

The Constraint-Driven Method™ does not minimize this reality. It accounts for it.

For single parents, integration requires heightened intentionality. Support systems are not optional; they are *infrastructure*. Childcare, family assistance, school resources, and institutional flexibility must be identified early and used deliberately. Attempting to absorb all demands alone is not resilience, it is exposure to breakdown.

Clarity in communicating with children is equally critical. Expectations and limitations must be named. Consistency matters more than availability. Children do not require perfection; they require stability, honesty, and reassurance that the relationship remains secure even when capacity is constrained.

Single parenting through law school is demanding. It is also possible. Success depends on rejecting isolation, planning aggressively, and treating support not as a personal shortcoming, but as a *strategic necessity*.

3.   THE INDICATORS YOU SHOULD FOCUS ON

Healthy parenting under constraint looks different—but it is no less real. Reliable indicators include:

- **Consistency over constant availability** Children know what to expect, even when schedules change.

- **Emotional safety** Children feel secure expressing needs, disappointment, or confusion without fear of rejection.

- **Clear communication** Expectations are explained in age-appropriate ways, including why certain seasons require adjustment.

- **Follow-through on commitments** When time is promised, it is honored—reinforcing trust.

- **Flexible routines** Structure exists but adapts to academic cycles and family needs.

- **Modeling perseverance and discipline** Children observe effort, responsibility, and purposeful sacrifice.

- **Healthy use of support systems** Caregivers, childcare, and community support are used without guilt or secrecy.

- **Repair after disruption** Missed moments are acknowledged and reconnected, rather than ignored.

- **Long-term stability over short-term perfection** Decisions are made by prioritizing sustainability over daily optics.

- **Preserved parent-child relationship** Law school is present in the household, but it does not replace love, attention, or identity.

The Constraint-Driven Method™ rejects the choice between being a good parent and being a high performing law student. Parenting is not an obstacle to overcome; it is a reality to be integrated. When guilt is removed from the equation, energy becomes available again for focus, execution, and endurance.

Parenting through law school is not easy. It is honest work. And it is work that can be done well.

This chapter strengthens the Constraint-Driven Method™ by removing guilt as a hidden drain on cognitive and emotional resources, allowing parenting responsibilities to be integrated into sustainable, high-performance practices.

18

CAREGIVING BEYOND PARENTING

Not all caregiving responsibilities involve children. Many law students provide ongoing care for elderly parents, disabled relatives, or family members with chronic needs. These responsibilities carry real time demands, emotional weight, and logistical complexity—often without the social recognition or institutional accommodation afforded to parenting.

The Constraint-Driven Method™ treats all caregiving as a legitimate operating condition, not a personal limitation. Whether care is provided to a child, an elder, or a dependent adult, the constraint is real and must be integrated into performance design rather than ignored.

Caregiving of this kind is often unpredictable. Needs arise without warning. Responsibilities cannot always be deferred. For students in these circumstances, planning must account for volatility, fatigue, and limited flexibility. Support systems, backup plans, and clear boundaries are essential.

Caregiving is a reality that requires strategic design. When a non-traditional student acknowledges this and integrates it honestly, their law school performance remains possible—even under sustained responsibility.

This chapter strengthens the Constraint-Driven Method™ by recognizing caregiving responsibilities as structural constraints and reframing them as conditions to be integrated into sustainable performance systems.

19

ACCESSING ACCOMMODATIONS EARLY

L aw school provides formal accommodations for students with documented needs, including learning differences, chronic health conditions, disabilities, and temporary impairments. These provisions exist as part of the institution's evaluation framework. They are *not* special treatment; they are mechanisms designed to ensure accurate assessment under standardized conditions.

However, many students who would benefit from accommodations either do not realize they qualify or delay seeking information until performance has already suffered. . By the time their needs become obvious, deadlines have passed, including the documentation requirements to qualify for accommodations, and their options narrow.

The Constraint-Driven Method™ treats accommodations as *infrastructure*, not contingency. If you suspect that time pressure, fatigue, processing speed, focus, or physical limitations materially affect your performance, you should investigate available accommodations *early*, even if you are unsure whether you will ultimately use them.

Accommodations often require:

- formal documentation
- advance approval

- coordination with faculty or administration

- lead time that cannot be compressed mid-semester

Waiting until there is a crisis eliminates leverage. Early inquiry preserves it. Using available accommodations does not change the standard. It allows the standard to be applied as intended. Law school exams measure legal reasoning under defined conditions; accommodations exist to ensure that evaluation reflects such reasoning rather than avoidable barriers.

If you receive accommodations and later determine they are unnecessary, nothing is lost. If you discover them too late, however, performance may already be compromised. Constraint-driven students gather information *before* they need it.

This chapter strengthens the Constraint-Driven Method™ by integrating institutional accommodations into performance design under constraint.

20

HEALTH AS CAPACITY INFRASTRUCTURE

Health is rarely discussed honestly in law school. When it is mentioned, it is often framed as self-care, balance, or personal responsibility. From a performance perspective, health is not a lifestyle choice. It is *capacity infrastructure*. Law school demands sustained cognitive effort, emotional regulation, and decision-making under pressure. Those demands are mediated through the body. When physical capacity degrades, performance degrades regardless of motivation, discipline, or strategy.

1.   HEALTH SETS THE CEILING ON PERFORMANCE

No system can outperform its limiting variable. Chronic sleep deprivation, unmanaged stress, inconsistent nutrition, or untreated physical conditions reduce:

- concentration

- memory consolidation

- emotional regulation

- recovery time

- judgment quality

When these capacities are compromised, students and the institution often misdiagnose the problem as lack of effort or resilience. Students attempt to compensate by working longer hours, increasing intensity, or cutting recovery further. But this accelerates decline.

From a constraint-driven perspective, this is a design failure, not a lack of grit. Health does not determine how hard a student works; it determines how much performance *is possible at all*. Recognizing this shifts health from a personal concern to a structural variable. Performance systems must therefore be designed to operate within physical limits, or they will fail under sustained pressure.

Effort cannot compensate indefinitely for physical depletion. A student may understand the material, apply the Method correctly, and still underperform if fatigue, illness, or chronic stress restricts cognitive capacity. At that point, performance does not fail because the strategy is flawed, but because the system has reached its biological ceiling.

Minimum Viable Health

The Constraint-Driven Method™ does not require optimal health. It requires *minimum viable health*.

Minimum viable health is the lowest level of physical functioning that still allows:

- clear thinking

- sustained attention

- emotional regulation

- and recovery after disruption

This threshold varies by individual and circumstance. The objective is not improvement for its own sake. The objective is to ensure that physical capacity does not become the limiting factor in system performance.

Minimum viable health generally includes:

- sufficient sleep to restore judgment

- sufficient nourishment to sustain focus

- sufficient movement to regulate stress

- sufficient medical or mental health support to avoid crisis

They are baseline requirements for system stability.

Health Is Non-Negotiable

Constraint-driven planning treats health the same way it treats time, caregiving, and work obligations: as a *fixed variable*.

If a system requires you to routinely violate your physical limits in order to function, the system is unsound. It may work briefly, but it will fail under pressure—often at the worst possible moment.

This is why health cannot be deferred until "after finals" or "after this semester." Deferred health becomes emergency health, which is far more disruptive and costly.

Sustainable performance requires accounting for physical health, not negotiating with it. Minimum viable health is preserved not through optimization, but through restraint. This includes:

- declining commitments that eliminate recovery time

- avoiding schedules that rely on chronic sleep loss

- recognizing when additional responsibilities create diminishing returns

- seeking medical or counseling support *early*, before crisis

None of these choices signal weakness. They signal system awareness.

Students who protect capacity maintain consistency. Students who ignore it oscillate between overwork and collapse.

2.   HEALTH IS NOT AN EXTRACURRICULAR

Health management is not something you add when time permits. It must be embedded in system design.

Constraint-driven students do not ask:

"How much can I push?"

They ask:

"What level of functioning must be preserved for this system to hold?"

That question keeps performance reliable across the semester, not just during strong weeks. Law school is not a sprint. It is a multi-year evaluative process followed by professional demands that do not ease simply because the degree is earned.

The goal of the Constraint-Driven Method™ is not peak output, but sustained, reliable performance over time. Minimum viable health makes that possible. Ignoring it is not a sign of commitment, rather it proves to undermine the outcomes students are working to achieve.

Under constraint, health is not a lifestyle concern but a structural limit that determines whether any performance system can hold over time.

21

PARTNERSHIP AS PERFORMANCE INFRASTRUCTURE

For purposes of this book, *partnership* refers to the functional relationship through which responsibilities, support, and decision-making are coordinated under constraint. Partnership may exist within committed structures, including marriage and professional partnerships.

Law school places sustained pressure on partnerships. That pressure does not arise because law school is incompatible with relationships, but because its demands are often left *undefined*. Strong partnerships are not built on proximity or convenience. They are built on shared understanding and shared purpose. When partners recognize law school as a finite, demanding, and consequential season, sacrifice becomes strategic rather than resentful. When that understanding is absent, even minor disruptions can feel personal and destabilizing.

---

1.   ENDURE FOR A SEASON

Law school is not forever. It is not worth the loss of durable relationships. It does not require abandonment of partnership; it requires clarity.

Partnerships usually deteriorate because of ambiguity, not workload. Sustaining partnership during law school depends on explicitly addressing:

- what law school demands

- what support realistically looks like

- which responsibilities must be redistributed temporarily

- which commitments remain non-negotiable

When these questions go unanswered, assumptions fill the gap. Left unchecked, assumptions harden into resentment.

During my first year of law school, my husband was deployed to Camp Humphreys, South Korea. There was no shared calendar, no daily check-ins, and no ability to redistribute responsibilities in real time. We were physically separated during one of the most demanding academic transitions of my life. Progress did not depend on ideal conditions. It depended on clarity, intentional support, and a shared understanding of the season.

Remember that stability is not always physical. For some families, stability is provisional rather than fixed. Military families, long-distance partnerships, and families managing unpredictable schedules operate without the assumption of shared space or synchronized routines. In these contexts, control over the environment is limited.

2.   DEFINE WHAT SUPPORT LOOKS LIKE FOR YOU

Support is not universal; it must be defined. In a partnership, support may come in different forms, such as:

- shared logistics

- visible presence

- emotional steadiness

- encouragement without distraction
- belief in your capacity

Support *must* be articulated, not assumed. Clearly define what support means to you and communicate it explicitly. Law school places strain not only on the student, but also on the partner absorbing secondary effects.

Hard seasons require unified direction. Do not treat partnership as something to manage around law school. That framing is backward. Partnership is indeed infrastructure. When it is intentional, it stabilizes everything else. When it is neglected, the cost surfaces academically, emotionally, and physically. Law school exposes weak systems quickly. Strong partnerships do not eliminate pressure. They absorb it.

You Should Not Do This Alone

Non-traditional students often pride themselves on self-sufficiency. Under sustained pressure, that instinct becomes limiting.

You do not need perfection in a partner but you do need support, emotional stability, shared alignment on priorities, and belief in your capacity. These are not optional. They are performance assets.

In marriage or professional collaboration, there will be moments when responsibilities must be delegated to preserve focus. Law school is demanding. Life does not pause. A functioning partnership is not a luxury, it is leverage.

Invest in Automation

Automation is not about comfort. It is about preserving capacity. Law school consumes time and attention aggressively. Laundry piles up. Rooms stay untidy. Dishes sit longer than you would like. Meals become inconsistent. Domestic systems degrade. This is not a failure of discipline; it is a structural consequence of sustained cognitive demand layered onto an already full life. If sufficient human support is unavailable, automation becomes necessary. This may include:

- a robot vacuum to reduce daily upkeep

- periodic cleaning services

- grocery delivery or meal services during peak academic weeks

- childcare or paid support for adults you care for

- outsourcing of tasks that do not require your judgment or presence

Some students address this constraint creatively. They might purchase gym memberships primarily because they offer on-site childcare that allow the student one or two uninterrupted hours to read, outline, or prepare. This is a typical example of strategic allocation of resources in service of sustained focus. Attempting to maintain pre-law-school domestic standards during law school often produces exhaustion, resentment, or guilt—none of which improve performance. Getting help is a must.

The Constraint-Driven Method™ treats energy as finite and attention as valuable. Tasks that do not require your skillset should not compete with those that do. Invest where you can. Automate where possible. Preserve your capacity for what only *you* can do.

This chapter supports the Constraint-Driven Method™ by treating partnership as strategic infrastructure that stabilizes performance and sustains execution under real-world constraints.

22

NETWORKING AS POSITIONING

Opportunity is not limited by geography. The legal profession operates across jurisdictions, borders, and platforms. Work and relationships ought to extend beyond the physical footprint of a student's law school.

The Constraint-Driven Method™ treats networking as life infrastructure. It must fit within responsibilities, respect energy limits, and align with long-term identity rather than short-term visibility. When designed correctly, networking does not compete with academic performance or personal stability.

---

1.   NETWORKING IS ABOUT POSITIONING

Networking does not replace competence. It complements it. Networking is about *positioning* yourself by building awareness, familiarity, and credibility in the spaces where you intend to operate after law school.

For students whose ambitions extend beyond the local market, waiting until graduation to establish these connections is unwise. Law school provides a rare window: you are credentialed, intellectually engaged, and expected to be learning. Global engagement fits naturally within that frame.

Constraint-Aware Networking Design

Traditional networking advice assumes:

- flexible schedules

- frequent in-person availability

- surplus energy

These assumptions rarely hold for non-traditional students. Constraint-aware networking is often lower cost and has a higher yield. It is typically asynchronous, selective, and content-driven rather than event-driven. This makes it compatible with constrained lives.

Constraint-driven relational capacity emphasizes:

- depth rather than volume

- alignment over visibility

- continuity instead of intensity

- contribution rather than extraction

The objective is not to accumulate contacts. It is to become reliably recognizable within the professional spaces that shape your future work.

Choose Relational Spaces Strategically

Not all spaces are worth engaging. Random networking does not produce durable opportunity.

Effective networking begins with role clarity. Ask:

- What type of work do I intend to do?

- In what regulatory, policy, or practice contexts?

- Within which industries, institutions, or issue areas?

Then identify the spaces where those conversations already occur. These may include:

- international professional associations

- cross-border practice groups

- academic or policy forums

- arbitration or compliance communities

- issue-specific conferences or working groups

- online platforms centered on substantive discourse

- training or research programs

Presence in these spaces should be purposeful. Do not try to be everywhere. Choose the networks where sustained attention will matter over time.

Contribution Precedes Connection

Networking is most effective when it is *contribution-based* rather than transactional. The truth is asking for attention without offering value rarely works. Contribution establishes credibility without requiring proximity.

Contribution can take many forms:

- thoughtful written commentary

- research assistance

- conference participation

- moderated engagement in professional forums

- collaborative projects aligned with your interests

These contributions need not be large, but they must be consistent and relevant. Over time, familiarity builds. Recognition follows.

2.   SEQUENCE LOCAL EXCELLENCE WITH GLOBAL AMBITION

Guardrails for Non-Traditional Students

Networking is not a substitute for performance. It is not a distraction from law school responsibilities. It must operate within clear boundaries. If your engagement:

- compromises academic performance

- destabilizes family or work obligations

- creates chronic stress

- or substitutes visibility for competence

it is misaligned with the Method.

Constraint-driven networking is additive. It fits within existing systems. It does not require overextension. The most effective non-traditional students do not choose between local excellence and global ambition. They sequence them correctly by:

- studying success locally to master evaluation systems

- networking globally to expand opportunity

- designing both deliberately rather than reactively

This approach reflects reality. Law school is local. Careers are not.

Global networking, when done with intention and restraint, allows non-traditional students to build futures that exceed the boundaries of their institutions.

Networking Should Be Evaluated on a Long Horizon

The benefits of networking are rarely immediate. Often, they are not visible during law school—or even in the years immediately following graduation. This does not make networking inefficient. It makes it strategic.

Non-traditional students are often impatient with activities that do not produce immediate payoff. Given limited time and energy, that instinct is understandable. In this context, however, it is misplaced. Networking is not an extracurricular activity. It is career infrastructure.

Professional relationships mature over time. Reputation builds quietly through consistency, judgment, and alignment. Being known as reliable and serious often proves more consequential than making a strong first impression. The value of networking is realized not through frequency of contact, but through continuity. Its returns are measured over years, not semesters.

Global networking is a strategy for students whose career trajectory goes beyond the local institutional market.

23

WORKING FULL-TIME AND STAYING COMPETITIVE

Working full-time during law school is not necessarily a disadvantage. It is a different operating condition. The problem is not employment. The problem is trying to study like someone who is *not* employed. That mismatch creates exhaustion, frustration, and unnecessary self-doubt.

---

1.   ADOPT PRECISION-BASED SYSTEMS

Students who work full-time must abandon volume-based study models and replace them with precision-based systems.

Time Is Not Your Most Valuable Resource

Most advice to working students focuses on time management. This is incomplete. Your most valuable resource is *cognitive energy*.

A student who studies six exhausted hours after work will underperform compared to a student who studies two focused hours with clarity and intent. Productivity is not measured in duration; it is measured in *output quality*.

Working students must protect their sharpest hours fiercely.

Do Not Try to Compete on Volume

Full-time workers cannot out-read, out-brief, or out-highlight tradi-tional students. Attempting to do so leads to burnout with no return. Competition in law school is not about who does the most. It is about who does *what matters*.

That requires:

- Studying for points, not pride

- Eliminating low-yield tasks

- Refusing performative busyness

2. WORK EXPERIENCE IS AN ASSET IF YOU USE IT CORRECTLY

Working students often underestimate what they contribute. Employ-ment sharpens:

- Time discipline

- Professional communication

- Stress tolerance

- Accountability

These skills translate directly into exam performance and writing qual-ity if you consciously apply them.

You already know how to meet deadlines, prioritize under pressure, and deliver when it counts. Law school simply requires those skills in a new format.

Set Non-Negotiable Academic Priorities

Working students must decide in advance which academic tasks cannot slip. These non-negotiable priorities typically include:

- Breaking down rules into elements and memorizing them
- Exam preparation
- Practice essays or performance tests under exam conditions
- High-yield review sessions

Everything else can be negotiable.

Perfection in readings, exhaustive note-taking, and endless supplementation are luxuries working students cannot always afford and do not need.

Communicate Strategically, Not Apologetically

You do not need to apologize for working.

When necessary, communicate clearly and professionally with professors or administrators about constraints. For example, if you need an extension to finish an assignment, state the constraint, explain the impact, and request the accommodation without guilt and without theatrics.

Do not overshare.
Do not seek sympathy.
Just be truthful.

Professionalism earns respect. Excuses invite doubt.

Fatigue Is Not Failure

There will be days when you are tired. That is not a character flaw. The mistake is interpreting fatigue as incapacity. Working students must distinguish between temporary exhaustion and strategic weakness. One requires rest. The other requires adjustment. Rest is not indulgence. It is maintenance.

You Are Already Training for Practice

Many law students struggle with the transition to legal work because they have never balanced competing demands.

Working students are already doing it.

Law school, employment, and life responsibilities simulate the pressures of legal practice. When managed intentionally, this experience becomes preparation, not penalty.

Competitiveness Is About Consistency

Staying competitive is not about peak performance every day. It is about reliable execution over time.

Working students win by:

- Designing sustainable systems
- Protecting recovery
- Showing up consistently
- Trusting the process

You do not need to match anyone else's schedule. You need to honor your own reality.

This chapter supports the Constraint-Driven Method™ by integrating full-time work into the performance system, ensuring employment obligations do not destabilize academic outcomes.

24

AFFILIATION GROUPS AND ASSOCIATIONS

Affiliation groups and student associations play a distinct role in law school. They can provide community, mentorship, institutional navigation, and a sense of belonging in an environment that often feels isolating. When utilized appropriately, they contribute to stability; however, when applied indiscriminately, they may further deplete limited resources.

The purpose of affiliation groups is not constant activity. It is *connection and access*.

For non-traditional students, these groups can offer:

- informal guidance on navigating law school culture

- exposure to alumni and practitioners

- shared understanding of lived experiences

- early insight into institutional norms and expectations

This form of social capital matters. But it does not require maximal participation.

1.   MEMBERSHIP IS NOT THE SAME AS OBLIGATION

A common mistake is assuming that joining an affiliation group requires attending every meeting, event, or initiative. That assumption turns a potential support system into a source of pressure.

It does not have to be that way.

Affiliation groups are most effective when approached with clarity:

- join with intention, not guilt

- attend selectively, not reflexively

- contribute when capacity allows, not at the expense of core responsibilities

Visibility does not require constant presence.

You must also choose groups that align with your goals. Not every group is for every student. Non-traditional students should prioritize associations that:

- reflect aspects of their identity or experience

- align with their professional interests

- provide access to mentorship or networks they would not otherwise have

Joining fewer groups with clearer purpose often yields greater benefit than joining many without direction.

2.   LEADERSHIP IS NOT MANDATORY

Leadership roles can be meaningful, but they are not required for affiliation groups to be valuable. For students already balancing work, family, or other obligations, leadership may add unnecessary strain.

There is no requirement to lead in order to belong.

Participation alone, when strategic, can still provide community, support, and access. It is up to you to decide whether a leadership role fits your circumstances.

Affiliation groups should reduce friction, not add to it. They are not measures of ambition or seriousness. They are one possible source of connection in a demanding environment.

3.   AFFILIATION GROUPS WORTH CONSIDERING

While offerings vary by school, the following groups often provide the highest return for non-traditional students. This list is illustrative, not prescriptive.

Professionally Oriented Associations

- Practice-area societies aligned with your interests (e.g., business law, public interest, criminal law, immigration law)

- Law and technology, health law, or international law associations

- Alternative dispute resolution or transactional law groups

These associations can provide early exposure to professional language, expectations, and career pathways.

Support and Navigation-Oriented Groups

- Non-traditional or evening/division-specific student groups

- Faith-based or values-based student organizations

- Bar association student chapters tied to your intended jurisdiction

These groups often serve as bridges between law school and the profession, offering practical guidance that is not always provided formally.

Identity- and Experience-Based Groups

- Student Parent or Caregiver Associations

- First-Generation Law Student Groups

- Military and Veterans Law Associations

- Women's Law Associations

- Black Law Students Association (BLSA)

- Latino/a Law Students Association (LLSA)

- Asian Pacific American Law Students Association (APALSA)

These groups often offer immediate cultural understanding, peer support, and informal mentorship. You do not need to join all or even many of these groups. One or two well-chosen affiliations can provide meaningful support without overwhelming your capacity.

A Three-Question Decision Filter

Before joining an affiliation group, ask yourself:

- Does this group provide access I would not otherwise have? (Mentorship, alumni connections, institutional insight, or professional exposure.)

- Does participation fit my current capacity without destabilizing core priorities? (Attendance and involvement should not compete with coursework, work, or family.)

- Is the value of this group clear without requiring constant presence or leadership? (If benefit depends on heavy involvement, this may not be the right season.)

The Constraint-Driven Method™ approaches affiliation groups as flexible supports that must fit within existing constraints, rather than commitments that compete with core execution.

The Constraint-Driven Method™ approaches affiliation groups as flexible supports that must fit within existing constraints, rather than commitments that compete with core execution.

25

2L ACTIVITIES: ALIGNMENT OVER ACCUMULATION

Once core obligations are accounted for, non-traditional students must decide what second-year activities to add. These activities are not requirements; they are elective commitments that should be evaluated only after core constraints are stabilized. Approached intentionally, they can add value. Approached reflexively, they often become unnecessary burdens.

1. 2L ACTIVITIES MUST ALIGN WITH GOALS AND CIRCUMSTANCES

The second year of law school is often presented as a checklist year. Students are encouraged to join journals, clinics, moot court, student organizations, and leadership boards—often simultaneously—under the assumption that more involvement automatically translates into better outcomes.

For non-traditional students, this framing is dangerous. Extracurricular involvement and professional activities are not inherently valuable; their value depends on whether they build competence, institutional credibility, or strategic positioning aligned with long-term goals.

Before committing to any 2L activity, ask a simple question: *What is this for?* Some activities build skills. Some signal interest to employers. Some provide community or meaning. Some do none of the above.

An activity that does not advance your goals, develop a needed competency, or support your professional direction is unlikely to justify its cost, especially when time and energy are already limited.

Common 2L Activities: Advantages and Tradeoffs

The activities below are not inherently good or bad. Their value depends entirely on *alignment*—with your goals, capacity, and constraints.

LAW REVIEW / JOURNALS

Advantages

- Signals strong academic performance

- Develops research, writing, and editing skills

- Well understood by employers

- Particularly relevant for clerkships, academia, and writing-heavy careers

Inconveniences

- Highly time consuming

- Deadlines often collide with exams

- Work is largely invisible and uncompensated

- Limited relevance for many paths

Best for: students pursuing clerkships, appellate work, or academic careers.
Risk: high workload with low flexibility.

CLINICS

Advantages

- Real client experience
- Practical skill development
- Clear professional relevance
- Often deeply meaningful

Inconveniences

- Time-intensive and unpredictable
- Client emergencies are not schedulable
- Emotional labor can be significant
- Reduced flexibility during peak academic periods

Best for: students who benefit from experiential learning and can absorb variability.
Risk: conflict with work, caregiving, or fixed schedules.

EXTERNSHIPS
Advantages

- Direct exposure to legal practice
- Networking
- Source for employment references
- Résumé credibility
- Clarifies career direction

Inconveniences

- Often unpaid
- Fixed hours and requires travel
- Adds workload without reducing academic demands

Best for: students who can integrate structured hours into existing commitments.
Risk: time compression and burnout.

MOOT COURT / TRIAL ADVOCACY

Advantages

- Develops oral advocacy and confidence

- Useful for litigation-focused careers

- Provides public performance experience

Inconveniences

- Rigid practice schedules

- Preparation time is often underestimated

- Competition seasons frequently overlap with exams

Best for: students pursuing litigation who benefit from performance-based learning.
Risk: time consuming with uncertain return.

STUDENT ORGANIZATION LEADERSHIP

Advantages

- Demonstrates leadership and initiative

- Builds peer and faculty relationships

- Can align with identity or career interests

Inconveniences

- Administrative workload

- Event planning demands

- Leadership responsibilities often expand unexpectedly

Best for: students with available bandwidth and clearly defined purpose.
Risk: leadership creep that drains capacity.

RESEARCH ASSISTANT POSITIONS

Advantages

- Close faculty interaction

- Skill development

- Potential recommendation letters

Inconveniences
- Deadlines depend on faculty schedules

- Workload can fluctuate unexpectedly

Best for: students interested in academic or research-heavy paths. **Risk:** lack of control over timing.

This list of 2L activities is not a checklist. It is a filter. An activity's advantage is irrelevant if its inconvenience destabilizes your life. Non-traditional students should not ask, *"Is this prestigious?"* but instead:

- Does this advance my stated goals?

- Can I absorb its inconvenience without compromising academics or family?

- Does this activity offer flexibility when disruption occurs?

Alignment beats accumulation. 2L is not about proving how much you can carry. It is about learning how to choose under constraint. Those habits—not résumés—are what transfer into practice.

An activity that creates chronic stress, strains family relationships, or competes directly with academic performance is not an achievement— it is a *liability*.

You should not accept commitments that become sources of constant pressure or recurring conflict. Strategic restraint preserves performance.

Involvement Can Be Strategic Without Being Excessive

This is not an argument for disengagement. It is an argument for *selective involvement*.

High-performing students choose roles that align with their goals, fit their circumstances, and add value without destabilizing the rest of their system. Doing fewer things well and consistently outperforms doing *many things poorly*.

Avoiding the Trap of Comparative Involvement

Much of the pressure around 2L activities comes from comparison. Students often measure themselves against peers who appear to be doing everything often without visibility into the costs. Do not confuse someone else's capacity, resources, or priorities with your own. What is manageable for one student may be unsustainable for another. Your law school journey is not a referendum on how much you can carry. It is an exercise in disciplined choice under constraint.

A Practical Rule

If an activity (1) advances your goals, (2) fits within your capacity, and (3) does not compromise your core obligations, it may be worth pursuing. If it does not, declining to engage in it is a strategic decision. The habits you form in law school, such as how you assess commitments, set boundaries, and protect your capacity will follow you into practice.

Choose accordingly.

Activities are not inherently valuable. They are tools. Like any tool, they are only useful when they serve a *defined* purpose.

2. WHAT CERTIFICATES AND SPECIALIZED PROGRAMS OFFER

Many law schools offer certificates or concentrations in specific subject areas such as alternative dispute resolution (ADR), business law, compliance, health law, intellectual property, or international law. Some schools also offer study abroad or international exchange programs for academic credit.

These opportunities can be valuable but only when evaluated realistically. Their value depends on how they align with your goals and capacity.

Certificates

Certificates add value when they:

- Demonstrate focused interest in a practice area

- Provide structured coursework in a specialty

- Offer access to specialized faculty or practitioners

- Can support certain career narratives (e.g., compliance, transactional work, ADR)

However, they:

- May require additional coursework beyond graduation minimums

- Can limit scheduling flexibility

- Do not always guarantee employment or specialization in practice

- Often matter less than grades, experience, or relationships

Certificates tend to be most useful when:

- they align directly with your intended practice area

- they do not require overloading your schedule

- they complement rather than compete with core academic performance

For non-traditional students, certificates should be evaluated as *optional* enhancements, not baseline expectations.

Study Abroad and International Programs

Some law schools offer short-term or semester-long study abroad opportunities. These programs provide cultural exposure, comparative legal perspectives, and unique academic experiences.

Their advantages are:

- Broader legal perspective

- Memorable academic experience

- Exposure to international or comparative law

- Networking with global institutions

Their inconveniences are:

- Significant cost

- Disruption to family, work, or caregiving responsibilities

- Limited relevance for many domestic practice paths

- Logistical complexity

Study abroad programs are best approached as intentional choices, not résumé fillers. For many non-traditional students, the opportunity costs—financial, relational, and logistical—are significant and may outweigh the professional return. These programs can offer perspective and intellectual enrichment, but they rarely function as direct performance multipliers in law school evaluation systems.

When pursued deliberately and with realistic expectations, study abroad experiences can provide distance from routine demands and exposure to different legal cultures. Their value lies less in credential accumulation and more in perspective, reflection, and contextual understanding. For students operating under constraint, the question is not whether such opportunities are inherently valuable, but whether they align with current priorities, capacity, and long-term goals.

Before committing to a certificate or study abroad program, ask:

- Does this advance my stated professional direction?

- Can I complete it without compromising grades, health, or family stability?

- Would the same time and resources yield greater return elsewhere (experience, networking, rest)?

Certificates and specialized programs can enhance your law school experience, but they are not substitutes for strong performance, clarity of purpose, or sustainable execution.

Under the Constraint-Driven Method™, alignment matters more than accumulation. Choose additions that strengthen your trajectory, not ones that merely expand your workload.

26

3L Year: Redeeming the Time

There is an old saying that most law students repeat: "1L, they scare you to death; 2L, they work you to death; and 3L, they bore you to death." Whether or not that is true is beside the point. The reality is that :

1Ls doubt they can succeed.

2Ls overextend everywhere.

3Ls waste valuable time.

Your final year is not a passive ending—it is your last controlled opportunity to shape what comes next.

---

1. Directing your Inputs

The last year of law school is the time where you have enough familiarity with the system to act deliberately and shape what comes next. It is not a year to drift. It is a year to execute and prepare for the transition beyond your final exam. Used strategically, this final year can define both your immediate next steps and your long-term trajectory.

Select Courses Strategically

Electives can reduce uncertainty. They allow you to test interests, develop targeted competencies, strengthen your résumé for specific employers, and make more informed decisions about your post-graduation trajectory.

Once your core doctrinal requirements are complete, you will gain control over your course selection. That control should be exercised with intention. At this stage, courses should serve one of two primary functions: (1) support your GPA objectives through favorable grading structures, or (2) build practice-relevant skills that translate into market value. Electives are not filler, nor are they simply a mechanism to reduce workload. They can shape your professional positioning.

For some students, this is the stage to deepen alignment with a defined practice area. A student pursuing criminal law may prioritize trial advocacy, evidence, sentencing, or prosecution clinics. A future business lawyer may focus on tax, securities regulation, mergers and acquisitions, or transactional drafting. A student interested in public interest work may select immigration clinics, family law practice, housing justice seminars, or mediation training.

For others, electives function as a testing mechanism. Doctrinal courses often present the law in abstract form; upper-level electives provide a closer approximation of practice.

Select Instructors Strategically

Each professor represents a different combination of access, credibility, and exposure. You should evaluate instructors with intention: their ability to write strong letters of recommendation, depth of expertise in your areas of interest, and reputation among students who have taken their courses.

Look beyond the syllabus. Courses that incorporate guest lecturers or adjunct faculty often provide direct access to practitioners with substantial experience in your target field. In some cases, these courses are offered infrequently, are highly competitive to enroll in, or are designed with a forward-looking perspective that aligns more closely with practice than doctrine.

The objective is not simply to learn the material. It is to position yourself through proximity, performance, and visibility.

Engage in Experiential Learning

Although non-traditional students often face structural barriers to accessing practical training, that gap has narrowed as the expansion of remote work has made experiential opportunities more accessible. You should treat this as a strategic advantage.

Pursue remote externships, clinics, symposiums, webinars, and seminars that provide direct exposure to practice when you can. Always prioritize opportunities that carry practical components—client interaction, drafting, observation of proceedings, or practitioner-led instruction. These are not peripheral activities; they are extensions of your professional development.

Where formal opportunities are limited, *create* access for yourself. Request to shadow practitioners, even for short, discrete periods. A few hours over several weeks can produce meaningful insight, strengthen professional relationships, and clarify your direction. Do not wait for structured programs to be offered. *Initiate* contact.

Your institution's career development office is an underutilized lever. Use it. Seek introductions to practitioners and alumni in your areas of interest. Be specific in your requests and clear about your objectives to target exposure to the environments you intend to enter.

If your institution offers academic credit for experiential work, incorporate it into your plan. For working students, this may include aligning current employment with qualifying legal tasks to convert existing commitments into credit-bearing activity. Where such programs do not exist, inquire. Institutional policies can be more flexible than they appear, particularly when approached with a well-defined proposal.

The objective is to ensure that your time in law school somewhat produces demonstrable, practice-relevant output, to the extent possible.

2. PUBLISHING YOUR LEGAL SCHOLARSHIP

Many law schools require a substantial research paper for graduation—often called a "long paper," "capstone," or "seminar paper." Typically, 30–50 pages, it is designed to demonstrate sustained analysis, doctrinal command, and original argument. A strong paper can be submitted for publication, support clerkship applications, or serve as a high-quality writing sample in the hiring process.

Selecting a Topic

A long paper is certainly not an extended exam answer. It is not a case summary or a compilation of sources. It is a structured argument that engages a legal problem, situates it within existing scholarship, and advances a clear, defensible position.

At minimum, it requires:

- A focused legal question

- A thesis that takes a position

- Sustained analysis supported by authority

- Proper citation and attribution

- Coherent organization over a significant word count

Topic selection is the first determinant of success. An effective topic sits at the intersection of three factors:

Interest – This paper is time-consuming; if you are indifferent about your topic, you may become reluctant to engaging with it and it may slow your progress.

Manageability – The issue you are addressing must generate enough answers to fulfill the page limit requirement.

Originality – The goal is contribution, not reinvention. Make sure you do a preemption check (confirming that your idea has not already been fully developed) so you do not duplicate work that already exists.

The practical and easiest approach for constraint-driven students is to:

- Choose a topic from the large pool of contentious issues at the executive level, the legislative level, or the judicial level

- Research sources for arguments both in favor of and against

- Take a strong stance

- Write a concurrence or a dissent

If you can clearly present an issue, provide a solution, and explain why, with great organization, you will end up with a near excellent research paper.

Selecting a Faculty Advisor

Some institutions require faculty supervision for your long paper. Where you can select your supervisor, your criteria should be strategic, not purely relational. Focus on subject-matter alignment, responsiveness, and clear expectations:

- Do they understand the area of your topic well enough to guide you?

- Do they provide timely feedback?

- Are their standards clear and consistent?

Before committing, you must clarify:

- Draft deadlines and feedback cadence

- Preferred communication style

- Level of substantive vs. structural guidance

A highly accomplished but unavailable faculty advisor creates unnecessary friction.

Working with a Librarian

Librarians are trained in advanced legal research beyond what is typically covered in class. They can help you navigate databases efficiently, trace authoritative sources, and determine whether your topic has already been addressed in existing scholarship.

Additionally, a librarian will guide you to the right sources early. Instead of spending hours searching broadly and inefficiently, you can be directed to:

- Key treatises and foundational texts

- Leading law review articles

- Relevant statutes, regulations, and case law

- Specialized databases you may not know exist

To engage with librarians effectively:

- Reach out early, before your topic is fully fixed

- Come prepared with a general area or research question

- Ask specifically for help with source mapping

- Clarify how to access and organize materials efficiently

A short, focused session with a librarian can replace hours of unstructured searching.

Writing and Editing on Time

Most long papers are delayed by poor sequencing. Treat the paper as a project with defined phases—topic selection early in the term, preliminary research and thesis development, a detailed outline, section-by-section drafting, and final revision with citation verification. Build the work in controlled segments that fit your actual schedule; consistency outperforms intensity. A concrete plan is essential.

Practical Example

- Convert the outline into writing tasks with clear timeframes (e.g., "write section II.B from 6 to 7 pm on Saturday 10/17" instead of "just work on paper tomorrow")

- Pair reading with immediate note integration to avoid re-reading sources

- Reserve specific sessions for citation work rather than mixing it into drafting

- Draft first, refine later (early perfectionism slows completion)

- Separate writing from editing (do not line-edit while generating analysis)

- Front-load structure (a strong outline reduces rewriting later)

Editing should occur in layers:

- Structural coherence (does the argument hold?)

- Clarity and transitions

- Citation accuracy and formatting

Plagiarism and Attribution

Long papers carry heightened academic integrity expectations.

Plagiarism is not limited to copying text:

- Cite as you write; do not defer attribution

- Keep clear records of sources

- Use quotation marks where appropriate

- When in doubt, cite

The Strategic Value of the Long Paper

For many students, the long paper is treated as a requirement to complete. However, it is one of the few opportunities in law school to develop an argument over time, refine it through feedback, and produce a finished work that can extend beyond the classroom.

If you intend to publish, timing and placement matter. Consult your institution's journals and law review early to understand submission cycles, editorial preferences, and whether priority is given to student members. Many journals fill a significant portion of their volume internally before opening to outside submissions, making late or uninformed submissions noncompetitive by default.

Where internal placement is limited, expand outward. Identify peer institutions with aligned subject-matter journals and track their submission windows. Treat this as a pipeline, not a single attempt.

Also consider alternative platforms. Practitioner-oriented publications, bar journals, and legal media outlets often accept shorter, adapted versions of long papers and may offer honoraria. These outlets typically prioritize clarity, timeliness, and practical relevance over purely academic framing.

3. PREPARING FOR PROFESSIONAL LICENSURE

The Bar Exam

One of the most abrupt transitions in legal education occurs immediately after your final exam. Law school ends, and bar preparation begins.

Many graduates underestimate how disorienting this shift can be. The bar exam is a distinct performance system—more demanding and less forgiving than most expect. It is the licensing examination required to practice law in a given U.S. jurisdiction and serves as the final gatekeeping mechanism between legal education and the profession.

Administered by each state, the exam assesses whether a graduate possesses the minimum competence to represent clients. It is typically offered twice per year, in February and July, over a two-day period, and requires a separate application process completed months in advance. Passing the exam alone is not sufficient for licensure; applicants must also satisfy character and fitness requirements and, in many jurisdictions, pass the Multistate Professional Responsibility Examination (MPRE).

3L year provides a window to prepare early. The goal is not to begin full bar study months in advance, but to make the structural decisions that will support it. This includes:

- Tracking bar application deadlines and requirements

- Understanding character and fitness obligations

- Budgeting for bar preparation and related expenses

- Planning time away from work, where feasible

- Identifying likely stress points before dedicated study begins

- Researching bar preparation programs and coaches, comparing approaches, evaluating costs, and deciding whether to study independently or with structured support

- Developing a realistic study plan that accounts for existing responsibilities, available time, and personal constraints

Not every law graduate is required to take the bar exam. The necessity depends on your intended role and jurisdiction. Positions that do not involve practicing law may not require licensure.

Some jurisdictions also offer alternative pathways, such as diploma privilege or admission on motion.

Be aware that professional development does not end with bar admission. Depending on career goals, additional certifications in compliance, privacy, project management, contract management, mediation, risk management, or other specialized fields may create opportunities beyond traditional legal practice. Researching these pathways during 3L year can help align post-graduation planning with long-term professional objectives.

The MPRE

You should account for the Multistate Professional Responsibility Examination (MPRE) as part of your 3L planning.

Many students complete the MPRE during their 2L year. If you did not, it becomes a timing issue, not just a testing requirement. The exam is offered three times per year—in March, August, and November—and delaying it can introduce unnecessary friction in the licensure process, even if everything else is in place.

3L year provides a final window to complete it without disrupting your post-graduation transition. This requires registering early, selecting a testing window—November or March of 3L year is often optimal—and avoiding conflicts with your heaviest academic or personal obligations. While not conceptually difficult, the MPRE is a separate performance requirement with its own timing and preparation demands.

Completing the MPRE during your last year ensures it does not become a bottleneck after your final exam, when your focus should shift to bar preparation and entry into practice.

4. DESIGNING YOUR POST-GRADUATION PATH

Graduation is not a single destination. It is a decision point. 3L year provides time to design what comes next, rather than react to uncertainty after finals.

For some graduates, the path is linear: bar exam, licensure, employment. For many, it is not. There is a multiplicity of paths available, between clerkships, firm roles, JD-advantage positions, compliance, policy, contract work, entrepreneurship, or paths outside traditional practice. The earlier these possibilities are examined, the stronger the transition becomes.

Designing a post-graduation path may involve updating application materials, strengthening professional networks, researching employers, initiating informational interviews, evaluating geographic markets, planning for financial stability during licensure delays, and identifying alternative pathways if timelines shift.

What kind of professional life are you trying to build?

What work structure fits your responsibilities?

What income timeline do you realistically need?

What risks can you absorb?

What version of success is attainable and sustainable for your actual life?

Answer before pressure sets in.

Under the Constraint-Driven Method™, deliberate preparation matters more than last-minute reaction. Build your final year in ways that strengthen your transition.

OPERATIONAL SUMMARY: PART V

This part requires you to protect the conditions that make sustained performance possible.

You are expected to manage life responsibilities as performance infrastructure, not distractions. That includes health, caregiving, work, relationships, and affiliations. The objective is not just balance. It is stability.

Before moving forward, you should have boundaries, routines, and support structures that prevent predictable breakdowns and preserve capacity during demanding periods.

PART VI — OUTCOMES & NEXT MOVES

"What we learn with pleasure we never forget."
—Alfred Mercier

27

What the Method Means for Legal Education

Legal education no longer operates exclusively within a single, traditional, full-time model. In the post–COVID-19 pandemic era, law schools have expanded delivery formats to include hybrid, blended, online, and extended-time programs. These models have increased access—and with it, the proportion of students operating under sustained external constraints.

1.   Beyond Access to the Law

Students enrolled in hybrid or blended programs are usually balancing employment, caregiving responsibilities, geographic constraints, or financial considerations alongside coursework. Even in traditional programs, asynchronous lectures, remote assessments, and flexible attendance policies have altered how and when students engage with material. What has not changed is how performance is evaluated.

Law school assessments remain time-bound, analytical, and comparative. Grading curves, exam formats, and institutional expectations continue to reward clarity, depth of analysis, and disciplined reasoning regardless of delivery format.

This matters because increased flexibility in access has not been matched by a corresponding shift in performance design guidance.

Why New Formats Increase the Need for System Design

Hybrid and online formats often assume that flexibility itself solves performance challenges. In practice, flexibility increases the burden of self-regulation. When structure is reduced, students must supply it themselves.

For students with margin, this may be manageable. For students operating under constraint, it is a little more of a risk.

Asynchronous lectures can accumulate. Boundaries between school, work, and home blur. Feedback cycles lengthen. There may be delays in guidance. Without deliberate system design, flexibility turns into diffusion, and diffusion undermines execution.

The Constraint-Driven Method™ addresses this reality directly. It does not rely on proximity, immersion, or excess availability. It assumes that students must perform across fragmented schedules, distributed environments, and competing obligations.

Format Does Not Eliminate Constraint

New delivery models do not eliminate constraint; they redistribute it:

- remote access may reduce commuting time while increasing isolation

- flexible scheduling may allow work continuation while compressing cognitive bandwidth

- online platforms may expand reach while obscuring evaluative signal

The Method is relevant because it is format-agnostic. It focuses on:

- identifying non-negotiable constraints

- clarifying evaluative signal

- designing execution systems that hold across contexts

- sustaining performance without relying on ideal conditions

As law schools continue to diversify their delivery models, the Method provides performance guidance adaptable to the evolving structure of legal education.

2.   BEYOND THE COMMON LAW

Although the discussion in this book is in the context of U.S. law schools, the conditions it addresses are not uniquely American. Across legal systems worldwide, students may enter law later in life, pursue legal education alongside employment or caregiving responsibilities, or navigate institutions without excess time, money, or flexibility.

Non-traditional law students are present in common law systems such as the United Kingdom and Australia, in hybrid systems such as South Africa, and in civil law jurisdictions such as France, even where educational pathways and exam formats differ.

What varies across jurisdictions is the *form* of legal education and assessment; what remains constant is the reality of evaluation under constraint. Legal training everywhere relies on structured reasoning, limited time, and human graders operating within institutional rules.

The Constraint-Driven Method™ is therefore not tied to any single exam format or doctrinal tradition. It is a framework for aligning preparation with how performance is actually evaluated in a given system. While its application must be adapted to local norms, the underlying logic—designing performance under real constraints rather than idealized assumptions—travels well.

The Constraint-Driven Method™ turns constraint into structure and sustains performance across formats and conditions.

28

How the Method Works as a Whole

High performance under constraint is not achieved by mastering isolated strategies. It depends on understanding how those strategies operate together.

The Constraint-Driven Method™ is not a checklist of tactics. It is an integrated system. Its effectiveness does not rest on any single principle, but on the way each component reinforces the others and compensates for the realities of a full life.

---

1.   The Method Is an Integrated System

Most academic advice assumes ideal circumstances. The Constraint-Driven Method™ is designed around reality.

Each principle the Method addresses includes a predictable pressure point: limited time and energy, delayed feedback, institutional opacity, stress, and informational noise. The Method does not attempt to eliminate these pressures. It structures performance so they no longer destabilize outcomes.

The system operates across three interdependent domains. None functions in isolation. Each enables and stabilizes the others.

Internal Endurance Sustains Execution

Endurance is not motivation; it is risk control. Knowing your why, recalling it under stress, and recognizing exhaustion before it distorts judgment prevent premature exits and self-sabotaging decisions. Without endurance, no strategy compounds long enough to produce results.

Performance Execution Converts Insight into Outcomes

Execution governs timing, focus, and allocation of effort. Staying ahead of predictable friction points, seeking help early, filtering noise, and repeating what works ensure that effort is directed where it yields returns. Most capable students lose ground not from lack of intelligence, but from inconsistent or misallocated execution.

Relational and Institutional Leverage Expands Margin

High performance does not occur in isolation. Institutions operate through gatekeepers, incentives, and informal rules. Peers and mentors provide calibration and stability. Understanding how people and systems function expands margin and amplifies the impact of sound execution.

Together, these domains form a system that holds under pressure.

2. WHY THE METHOD WORKS UNDER CONSTRAINT

The Constraint-Driven Method™ works because it aligns with how performance actually unfolds in real life.

- Endurance prevents collapse

- Execution prevents waste

- Leverage prevents isolation and misalignment

The Method reduces volatility. It stabilizes performance across semesters, courses, and evaluators. It allows non-traditional students to compete not by doing more, but by doing what matters consistently.

Importantly, the Method is iterative. Each semester refines the system. Strategies are repeated, adjusted, and improved. Over time, performance becomes more predictable and less fragile.

When the Method is operating as designed, several shifts occur:

- Confusion is addressed earlier

- Study time becomes more efficient

- Feedback is filtered more intelligently

- Stress becomes manageable rather than paralyzing

- Results improve without proportional increases in effort

At this point, performance no longer feels reactive. You are not responding to law school as it happens; you are operating within it deliberately.

From Law School to Life

Although this book applies the Constraint-Driven Method™ to law school, the Method itself is *not* confined to legal education. Any environment defined by high stakes, delayed feedback, and fixed constraints can be navigated using the same logic.

That transferability is intentional. The Method was built to continue to be of use beyond a single institution or season.

The Constraint-Driven Method™ functions as an integrated system—converting endurance into execution, execution into leverage, and leverage into sustained, repeatable performance.

29

What High Performance Looks Like Under Constraint

High performance under constraint does not depend on eliminating interference. It assumes the opposite. Non-traditional students do not operate with unlimited time, uninterrupted focus, or the ability to reorganize life around academics, and high performance does not require acquiring those conditions.

---

1. Design Performance Based on Real Conditions

Under constraint, effectiveness comes from design. Constraints are not eliminated. They are anticipated, managed, and neutralized through strategy. The goal is not frictionless execution. It is sustained effectiveness despite friction.

This is why consistency matters more than intensity. Students with full lives rarely have access to prolonged bursts of effort. What they can maintain when systems are properly designed is *rhythm*.

High-performing students under constraint typically:

- work in shorter, focused intervals

- return to material consistently rather than cramming

- prioritize follow-through over ambition

- preserve momentum when schedules are disrupted

This is not a compromise. It is a superior design for real-world conditions. Progress under constraint is cumulative. It becomes visible across time, not in isolated moments. Performance improves as alignment increases.

Common indicators include:

- steady improvement across assessments

- fewer preventable errors

- clearer alignment with evaluators

- increased efficiency in preparation

- greater confidence in execution

Stress and fatigue may still occur. What changes is that performance continues *despite* them.

2.   SHIFT FROM REACTION TO RELIABILITY

As systems replace guesswork, effort becomes strategic rather than reactive. High-performing students under constraint do not wait for problems to surface before responding. They:

- seek clarification before confusion escalates

- address weaknesses before exams expose them

- filter advice based on authority

- repeat effective strategies instead of reinventing approaches

High performance is not doing everything. It is doing what matters at the right time.

One of the clearest signs that the Method is working is a *reduction in chaos*. When execution is deliberate, outcomes stabilize.

It often looks like:

- improved grades without proportional increases in study time

- fewer last-minute emergencies

- reduced emotional volatility around assessments

- greater confidence in decision-making

Law school remains challenging but becomes manageable. The most significant shift is internal. Students stop experiencing law school as survival and begin experiencing it as execution.

They no longer ask: *"How am I going to get through this course?"*

They begin asking: *"How do I want to run this course?"*

That shift—from reaction to control—is a hallmark of the Constraint-Driven Method™.

Grades Are Not Your Final Verdict

Law school grades reflect how well a student performed under defined constraints relative to a particular peer group. They should be taken seriously. But they do not capture the full scope of a student's capacity, nor do they determine the trajectory of future success.

It is not uncommon for students who never earn an A in law school to go on to build successful, even exceptional, legal careers—including thriving solo practices, respected boutique firms, and influential roles outside traditional firm hierarchies.

This outcome is not anomalous, nor does it reflect a failure of legal education. It just reflects the limits of what law school evaluation is designed to measure.

Law school grades assess performance under a narrow set of conditions that reward certain skills with precision. They do not fully capture other competencies that later prove decisive, such as client development, judgment under uncertainty, risk tolerance, negotiation, business acumen, adaptability, or long-term execution.

As a result, academic performance and professional performance are correlated but not synonymous.

Understanding this distinction is critical when interpreting outcomes. A transcript is a data set, not a *prophecy*. It reveals strengths, gaps, and patterns of execution within law school's evaluative framework. It does not dictate the scope of your professional ceiling.

This does not mean grades should be dismissed. It means they should be *interpreted strategically*.

Students who struggle academically but later excel professionally often do so because they develop systems that law school does not test directly: resilience over long horizons, client trust, operational discipline, and the ability to execute consistently in ambiguous, real-world conditions. Conversely, strong academic performers who fail to adapt beyond law school sometimes misinterpret early success as a comprehensive indicator of future dominance.

The Constraint-Driven Method™ is designed to prevent both errors.

When outcomes are viewed correctly, grades become what they were always meant to be: informative signals, not identity statements or final judgments. Used well, they guide adjustment. Used poorly, they distort decision-making.

Constraint-driven students design law school performance as part of a broader trajectory, ensuring that effort serves not only grades, but long-term endurance, transferable skill, and strategic positioning.

3. What High Performance Does Not Require

High performance under constraint does *not* require:

- sacrificing health or relationships

- isolation or constant comparison

- suffering as proof of seriousness

- outperforming everyone, everywhere

It requires alignment. It requires repetition. It requires restraint.

The outcome is *reliability*.

You become someone who produces solid results consistently, even when conditions are *imperfect*. That reliability builds confidence with evaluators, credibility within institutions, and self-trust over time.

High performance is not accidental. Under constraint, it must be *designed*.

This chapter defines the measurable and experiential outcomes of the Constraint-Driven Method™, showing how disciplined design and consistent execution produce reliable performance.

30

APPLYING THE METHOD BEYOND LAW SCHOOL

Although this book applies the Constraint-Driven Method™ to law school, the Method itself was never meant to be confined to legal education. Law school is simply one of the clearest environments in which constraint, delayed feedback, high stakes, and institutional opacity converge. Those conditions are not unique. They recur across professional careers, leadership roles, caregiving, entrepreneurship, and any environment where performance matters but ideal conditions are unavailable. The Method works because it is built for *reality*—not for a single institution. This is how the Method™ carries forward.

1.   WHY THE METHOD TRANSFERS

The Constraint-Driven Method™ does not depend on subject-matter expertise. It depends on *structure*.

Across environments, the same operational challenges repeat:

- limited time and energy

- delayed or opaque evaluation

- competing responsibilities

- gatekeepers and discretionary decision-makers

- information overload and noise

The Method transfers because it addresses these conditions at the level where failure actually occurs: system design.

You are not learning how to succeed in law school. You are learning how to design performance under constraint in general.

The core logic remains consistent wherever stakes are high.

Endurance Comes First

Whether in legal practice, organizational leadership, career transition, or caregiving, performance collapses without internal stability. Knowing your purpose, revisiting it under pressure, and recognizing exhaustion before it distorts judgment prevent premature exits across domains. Burnout is rarely a character flaw; it is more often a design failure.

Execution Determines Outcomes

Results are produced through timing, focus, and repetition, not raw effort. Outside law school, the same execution principles apply:

- clarify expectations early

- anticipate friction before it escalates

- filter out non-authoritative input

- repeat strategies that produce results and adapt them deliberately

High performers do not indefinitely chase novelty. They *refine* execution.

Leverage Exists Everywhere

Every system distributes opportunity through incentives, discretion, and informal rules. Beyond law school, gatekeepers may be supervisors, clients, regulators, investors, or institutional leadership.

The titles change.
The function does not.
Those who understand how evaluation actually occurs gain margin others never access.

The Method works because it mirrors reality.
It does not assume control.
It assumes constraint and designs accordingly.

2. THE TRANSITION TO THE NEXTGEN BAR EXAM

The transition to the NextGen Bar Exam further underscores the relevance of performance systems designed for constraint.

The NextGen framework places increased emphasis on applied skills, integrated legal analysis, and performance across realistic scenarios rather than isolated memorization. It reflects a broader shift in legal education and licensure: evaluation is moving closer to how lawyers *actually* reason and perform under pressure.

What has not changed is the underlying challenge. Candidates must still convert limited time, energy, and cognitive bandwidth into reliable performance within a high-stakes evaluative system.

The Constraint-Driven Method™ aligns naturally with this evolution. Its focus on signal identification, execution design, and sustainability prepares students not only for doctrinal exams, but for applied assessment environments that reward judgment, prioritization, and disciplined reasoning.

As law school curricula and licensure models evolve, the advantage will belong to those who operate from systems that hold across formats. The Method is not bar specific. It is performance-specific and therefore durable across assessment regimes.

3.   CARRYING THE SYSTEM FORWARD

What makes the Constraint-Driven Method™ durable is repetition. Once you identify what works, progress accelerates when you:

- preserve the core structure

- adapt execution to new conditions

- resist unnecessary reinvention

This is how competence becomes reliability—and reliability becomes mastery. The Method does not require you to reinvent yourself in each new environment. It gives you a stable operating system that travels with you.

Constraints will change.
Responsibilities will shift.
The structure remains.

As you move beyond law school, carry forward:

- a commitment to designing accounting for constraints rather than denying them

- a discipline of early clarification

- an intolerance for wasted effort

- an understanding of institutional dynamics

- a bias toward refinement over experimentation

These are not academic habits. They are operating principles.

Law school may be the first environment in which you apply the Constraint-Driven Method™, but it need not be the last. Over time, the Method evolves with you.

4.   FROM PERFORMANCE TO IMPACT

When systems become reliable—when capacity is protected, execution is consistent, and outcomes are no longer fragile—contribution becomes possible without self-sacrifice.

Giving back is not a moral obligation or a test of seriousness. It is a function of capacity. This distinction matters. When contribution is expected before stability exists, it produces depletion rather than impact.

Under the Constraint-Driven Method™, contribution follows performance; it does *not* precede it. Once stability is established, contribution serves a strategic function.

Teaching reinforces mastery.
Mentorship clarifies systems.
Institutional engagement expands leverage—not only for you, but for those who follow.

Contribution may take many forms.

You may support incoming students by helping them avoid predictable mistakes and decode institutional expectations.

You may strengthen alumni networks or affinity groups that improve access and transparency. You may engage more broadly, modeling disciplined ethical participation within the profession.

What matters is not the form of contribution, but its alignment. Make sure you maintain clarity, selectivity, and leverage.

At its best, contribution multiplies impact. It converts individual success into shared advantage. It improves systems for those who come next—not through sacrifice, but through design.

This is where performance extends beyond personal outcomes. When execution is stable and leverage is available, excellence becomes transferable.
Knowledge becomes infrastructure.
And success, properly designed, does not end with you.

This chapter demonstrates the portability of the Constraint-Driven Method™, showing how its architecture applies to any high-stakes environment governed by limited resources, delayed feedback, and institutional complexity.

31

SYSTEM REVIEW

When graduates are asked what they would change if given the chance to start law school again, many say they would change nothing. I would change a great deal. Law school is often understood only in hindsight once the pieces finally connect.

Clarity frequently arrives after the cost has already been paid—in time, energy, and unnecessary stress. The purpose of the Constraint-Driven Method™ is to shorten that delay, allowing students to act on clarity before paying for it.

This chapter identifies which decisions reinforce performance under constraint and which adjustments stabilize it sooner.

1. WHAT HOLDS

When capacity is limited, you should prioritize short-horizon stability. This involves protecting execution, preserving margin, and preventing system breakdown. Once performance becomes reliable, you can shift your attention to longer-horizon positioning.

Effective design requires knowing which horizon governs the decision in front of you—and resisting the pressure to optimize both when constraint makes that impossible.

The following decisions consistently support reliable performance:

- *Engaging evaluators early and intentionally.* Performance improves when expectations are clarified before stakes escalate. Early alignment reduces rework and uncertainty.

- *Building a law school village deliberately.* Academic and emotional infrastructure reduces isolation and preserves judgment under pressure.

- *Setting clear performance goals and remaining committed to them.* Consistency matters more than recalibration. Stability supports execution.

- *Persisting through difficulty without reinterpreting struggle as failure.* Discomfort functions as information, not diagnosis.

- *Seeking help repeatedly and early.* Support operates as leverage rather than remediation.

Collectively, these decisions reduce variance and allow strategies to yield reliable results over time.

2. WHAT ADJUSTS

The following adjustments stabilize performance as they align more strictly with constraint-driven design:

- *Trusting non-linear progress.* Early positive results matter less than sustained momentum. Perfection is unnecessary but direction is decisive. You should pursue excellence, not perfection.

- *Incorporating the reality of constraints sooner.* Resistance wastes energy. Designing with reality preserves it.

- *Detaching emotionally from doctrine.* Law school rewards analysis, not absorption. Emotional overinvestment reduces focus without improving outcomes.

- *Stopping the over-preparation of low-yield tasks.* Effort must be judged by return, not by how productive it feels.

- *Filtering opinions aggressively.* Peer advice often lacks context. Professor feedback and institutional signals deserve priority.

- *Trusting pace over comparison.* Progress becomes clearer when measured against system performance rather than peer timelines.

- *Protecting sleep without guilt.* Exhaustion distorts judgment more often than it reveals deficiency.

- *Networking early and with intention.* Local mastery supports evaluation; broader networking expands opportunity.

- *Using supplements consistently rather than sporadically.* Deliberate use improves efficiency; intermittent use introduces noise.

- *Preparing for post–law school early.* Career positioning benefits from lead time, not last-minute correction.

- *Eliminating activities without downstream value.* Alignment matters more than accumulation.

- *Leveraging mentorship, academic and professional, early.*

- *Practicing under exam conditions sooner and more often.* Execution improves only through repetition.

- *Choosing electives strategically.* Courses with favorable grading structures and practical relevance produce stronger returns.

- *Taking bar-preparation courses even when optional.* GPA and bar readiness solve different problems. Early exposure reduces later strain.

Each adjustment reinforces the same lesson: performance stabilizes when design replaces optimism. This review clarifies what endures and what adjusts; the final responsibility now shifts to you—to apply these principles deliberately, under your own constraints.

The Constraint-Driven Method™ exists so these lessons do not have to be learned through trial and error. It allows students to operate with foresight instead of hindsight—using structure to avoid unnecessary cost.

OPERATIONAL SUMMARY: PART VI

This part requires integration.

You are expected to step back and evaluate what holds, what adjusts, and how the Method transfers beyond law school. High performance under constraint is not situational—it is portable.

Before proceeding, you should be able to articulate how your systems function as a whole, how they adapt as circumstances change, and how stabilized performance can translate into broader impact.

PART VII — SELECTED PERFORMANCE EXECUTION TOOLS

"Plans are only good intentions unless they immediately degenerate into hard work."

— **Peter Drucker**

T his section includes selected tools to illustrate how the Constraint-Driven Method™ is operationalized in practice. These examples demonstrate how strategy becomes repeatable execution under real constraints. They are not exhaustive, nor are they intended to replace judgment, adaptation, or system design.

The purpose of these tools is not completion for its own sake. Their purpose is to reduce decision fatigue, stabilize execution, and translate strategic clarity into action.

CONSTRAINT MAPPING TEMPLATE

Purpose: Identify fixed realities so planning is honest and executable.

This template demonstrates how constraint-aware design translates strategy into execution. It is designed to be used for each semester. Adapt as needed based on your context.

A. Fixed Constraints (Non-Negotiable This Semester)

☐ Work hours

____

____

____

☐ Caregiving responsibilities

____

____

____

☐ Commute / location limits

____

☐ Health / energy limits

☐ Financial constraints

☐ Others

These are inputs, not excuses.

B. Flexible Variables (Should Be Adjusted)

☐ Study timing

☐ Study location

☐ Resource(s) selection

☐ Social commitments

☐ Perfection standards

☐ Others

C. Design Decision

Given these constraints, success this semester looks like:

Weekly Study System Template

Purpose: Prioritize outcomes over hours.

This template illustrates how weekly execution is structured around evaluation, not effort.

A. Non-Negotiable Academic Outputs This Week/Month/Semester

(What earns points)

____

____

____

____

____

____

____

B. High-Yield Tasks (Do First)

☐ Reading assignments

☐ Outline

☐ Memorize rules

☐ Practice essays / Multiple choice questions

☐ Professor-specific preparation

☐ Other

____

____

C. Low-Yield Tasks to Minimize (Do Second)

☐ Reading supplements

☐ Briefing

☐ Other

____

____

D. Best Cognitive Windows

☐ Peak focus time(s):

____

____

☐ Backup window(s):

____

____

E. Weekly Reality Check

If this week collapses, the three things I will still complete are:

EXAM DECODING FRAMEWORK

Purpose: Study for *this* exam, not exams in general.

This framework demonstrates how preparation is reverse engineered from grading mechanics.

A. Professor & Course

☐ Professor/Course/Strategy

B. Exam Structure

☐ Issue-spotter

☐ Essays

☐ Multiple Choice Questions

☐ Open / Closed book

☐ Time-pressured or Not

C. What This Professor Rewards Most

☐ Issue volume

☐ Depth of analysis

☐ Rule precision

☐ Organization

☐ Policy discussion

D. Common Traps / Emphases

E. Study Strategy Alignment

Based on this exam, I will prioritize:

PROFESSOR OUTREACH SCRIPTS

Purpose: Communicate strategically within institutional structures.

These scripts demonstrate how clarity and professionalism reduce friction and improve alignment.

A. Professor Outreach Scripts

Hello Professor [Name],

I am preparing for [exam/assignment] and wanted to confirm that my approach to [specific issue] aligns with your expectations. Would you recommend I focus more on [option A] or [option B]?

Thank you for your time, [Name]

B. Exam Clarification Question

Professor [Name],

As I prepare for the final, I want to ensure my analysis is aligned with your grading priorities. On essays, is it more important to identify all plausible issues or to deeply analyze the most significant ones?

Respectfully, [Name]

C. Post-Assessment Feedback Request

Professor [Name],

I have reviewed my [exam/assignment] and would appreciate your insight into one area in which I could improve for future assessments. I am particularly interested in how I could strengthen my [analysis/organization].

Thank you, [Name]

OPERATIONAL SUMMARY: PART VII

This part requires application on your part.

You are expected to use the tools provided not as templates to copy, but as structures to adapt. Tools are only valuable when they fit your constraints and support execution reliably.

Before concluding this book, you should have at least one system mapped, one workflow stabilized, and one point of execution improved measurably.

CONCLUSION

This book began with a simple but often unspoken truth: law school was not designed for people with full lives. It was built around assumptions—that law school students have flexible schedules, minimal external obligations, and uninterrupted focus—and these assumptions do not reflect the realities many students face today. For non-traditional students, the assumptions are not merely inconvenient. They are structurally misaligned.

The problem, however, is not law school itself. The problem is how to approach law school.

This book has rejected the idea that success requires becoming an "ideal" student. Instead, it settles for something more realistic and more effective: a strategy designed around the student and its own circumstances.

That is the purpose of the Constraint-Driven Method™.

What This Book Has Shown

High performance under constraint is neither accidental nor reserved for those with fewer responsibilities. It is a product of deliberate design. You were introduced to a system organized around three strategic layers:

- *Internal Endurance*, which prevents premature exit

- *Performance Execution*, which converts effort into results

- *Relational and Institutional Leverage*, which expands margin and amplifies outcomes

Each principle addressed a predictable pressure point—burnout, misdirection, institutional opacity, wasted effort, isolation. None functioned in isolation. Each reinforced the others. Together, they form an operating system for high performance under constraint.

What Changes When the System Is in Place

When the Constraint-Driven Method™ is applied consistently, several shifts occur:

- confusion is addressed earlier

- effort is allocated more efficiently

- feedback is filtered more intelligently

- performance stabilizes across semesters

- stress becomes manageable rather than paralyzing

Law school does not become easy. It becomes navigable. It becomes manageable.

Most importantly, students stop reacting to law school and begin operating within it deliberately.

What This Book Did Not Promise

This book did not promise perfection. It did not promise effortlessness. It did not promise freedom from stress or sacrifice.

What it offered instead was control to the extent possible:

- control over how time and energy are allocated

- control over which voices are prioritized

- control over when to seek help and how to use it

- control over repetition, refinement, and execution

Under constraint, control is the real advantage.

From Law School Forward

Although this book applied the Constraint-Driven Method™ to law school, the Method is not limited to this context. Law school is simply one of the clearest environments in which high stakes, delayed feedback, fixed constraints, and institutional complexity intersect.

Those conditions exist elsewhere.

The value of the Method is that it carries forward. As responsibilities shift and environments change, the structure remains. You learn to design performance around reality rather than resisting it.

A Final Word

Most performance systems are designed for people with margin. The Constraint-Driven Method™ is designed for people without it.

Performance under constraint is not about effort, resilience, or sacrifice for their own sake. It is about alignment—between goals, conditions, and execution.

The life you have is not an obstacle to overcome. It is the reality within which performance must be built.

When performance is designed around reality rather than against it, results stabilize, judgment sharpens, and progress becomes repeatable.

That is the purpose of the Constraint-Driven Method™: a repeatable system for high performance when ideal conditions do not exist.

Performance under constraint is not accidental. It is designed.

If you do not turn your constraints into strategic inputs that shape your success, they will become excuses that justify your failure.

ACKNOWLEDGMENTS

Without Him, I can do nothing—Jn 15:5

I wrote this book for individuals who carry real responsibility and still choose to pursue excellence.

Thank you to my family for the sacrifices that made this journey possible.

To my children: you were never the reason I could not do it—you were the reason I had to.

To my husband: thank you for loving us through it all, especially through seasons of distance and change. Your leadership has always been fruitful.

Thank you to the mentors, professors, and administrators who offered guidance, clarity, and dignity at the moments it mattered most.

Thank you to the classmates and friends who formed the village that made the pressure bearable.

Thank you to those who provided shelter, support, and prayer during critical transitions, especially Uncle John Riediesel—your generosity made completion possible.

Most of all, thank you to the reader.

If you are holding this book while carrying a full life, I hope it gives you what most systems do not: a strategy designed for reality.

Contact & Resources

For Institutions and Academic Programs

The Constraint-Driven Method™ is available for structured institutional implementation.

While this book introduces the conceptual architecture and student-facing application of the Method, formal adoption involves defined implementation standards, faculty briefing modules, readiness assessments, and structured integration pathways designed for academic environments.

Institutions interested in pilot programming, authorized implementation, faculty training, or strategic consultation are invited to make direct inquiry.

Additional Resources

Updates, supplemental materials, and future developments related to the Constraint-Driven Method™ may be made available at:

www.constraintdrivenmethod.com

A companion digital platform and mobile application designed to support implementation of the Method—including performance tracking, study system design, and constraint-mapping tools—will be introduced in the future. Information regarding availability and access will be provided through the website.

For professional correspondence, speaking engagements, media inquiries, or institutional partnerships, please contact:

hello@constraintdrivenmethod.com

Readers interested in ongoing developments, implementation resources, or future publications connected to the Method are encouraged to visit the website periodically for updates.

Readers interested in connecting with the author directly are encouraged to visit www.linkedin.com/in/constraintdrivenlawyer.

273